# On Modern German Literature

# On Modern German Literature

PAUL KONRAD KURZ, S. J.

Volume III

*English translation by*
Sister Mary Frances McCarthy

THE UNIVERSITY OF ALABAMA PRESS
*University, Alabama*

On Modern German Literature

Volume I Published 1970

Volume II Published 1971

Volume III Published 1972

Volume IV Forthcoming 1973


ISBN 0–8173–8002–7
Library of Congress Catalog Card Number 73–96419

Manufactured in the United States of America

# *Table of Contents*

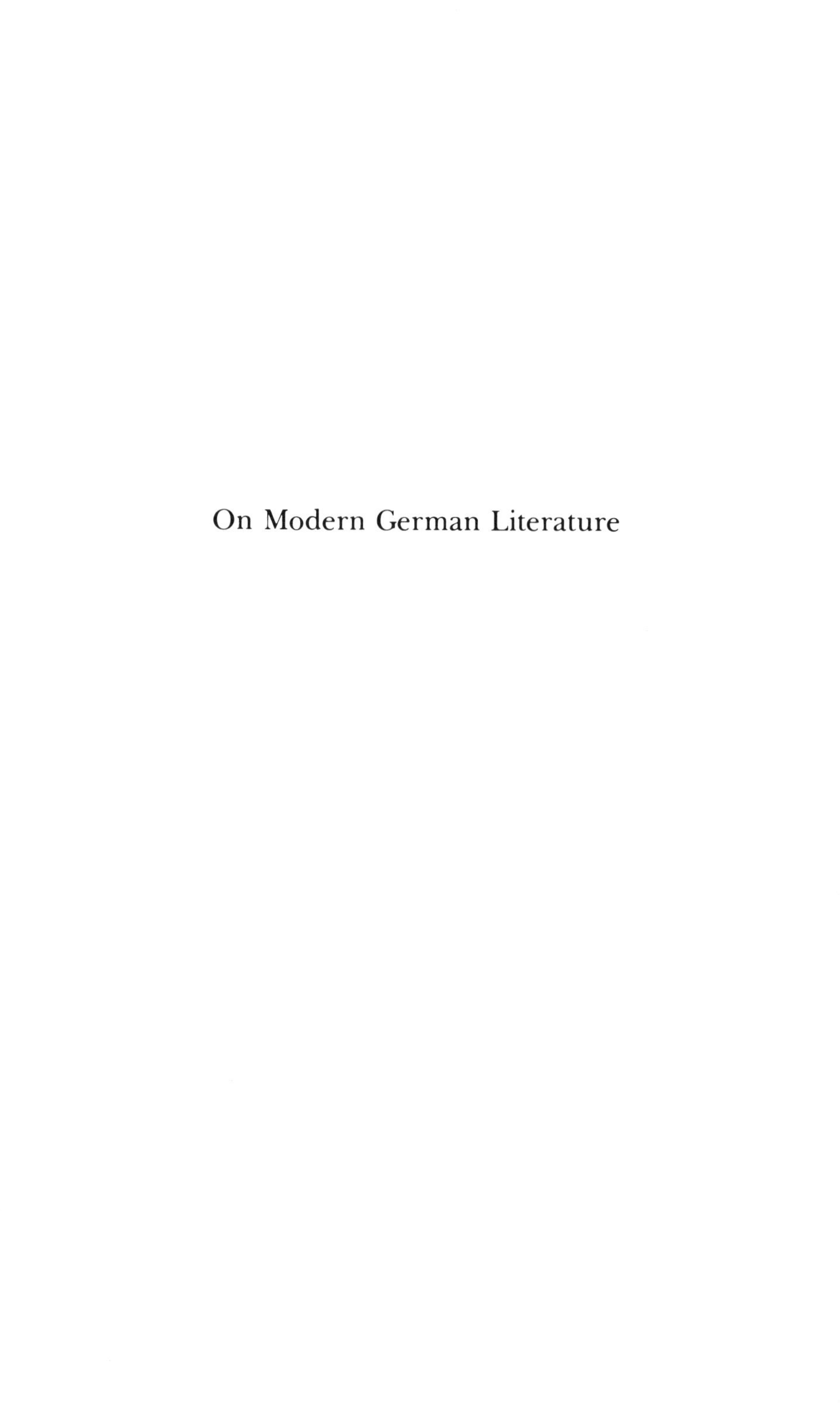

# On Modern German Literature

Many Christians regard contemporary literature with skepticism. Many writers regard Christians with skepticism. Whoever attempts to come to terms with both groups ends by pleasing neither. But perhaps pleasing is not the first thing to be considered.

# 1

# *The Individual's Awareness of Self and World As Manifested In German Lyric Poetry Since 1945*

## *From the Sublime to the Anti-Icarus*

For some years now, people have been aware that modern lyric poetry gives no less adequate expression to the intellectual situation of the present than do philosophy, theater, novels, or painting. People are aware that "great poems have the value of documents" (Brecht). They are aware that some lyricists of the present century have betrayed the moon, no longer hearken to the nightingale, allow no fountains to splash except in *terza rima*, and pay no homage at the pedestals of sonnets. The older writers bowed their heads in elegiac mood. More recent ones have urged their cause with dissatisfaction and revolutionary zeal. Some of the most recent shoot out tongues of satire and parody. In this century, lyric poetry has changed in many respects. Goethe's "evening," Mörike's "beautiful lamp," C. F. Meyer's "late boat" are beyond recall. No one can settle now in Eichendorff's woods, in George's parks, in Hofmannsthal's avenues, in Rilke's inner space of the world. Trakl's blackbirds have given place to Grass's hens and Enzensberger's crows.

From decade to decade in the twentieth century, the world has been more and more depoetized. And with the depoetizing of the world, the poetic reflection, the poem, has had to change. Where nightingales and blackbirds once sang, there is now the roar of airplanes. Airplanes are frameworks covered with montages. The construction and parts of "modern" poems are also like frameworks covered with montages. One whose lyric taste was schooled on the works of Goethe, Eichendorff, or Rilke finds disappointment today on every side. The poem has changed because the individual who speaks and constructs lyrics has changed: his supporting leg, his balance, his outstretched arms, his dress, his intercourse with ancestors, machines, taboos; his process of demythologizing; his grasp of the demythologized world; his emancipation that oscillates between power and powerlessness; his feelings of agression against an amorphous society; his repressions and his outbursts; his courage and his lack of courage before the face of the God Who has been dismissed; his doubts about the total construction of his own household. If we want to survey their terrain, it is not our feelings which we must examine first, but our perception; not our attention to space and our interest in it, but the way in which others keep their floors clean and their houses in order.

The lyric games are not dead, but banned: from the parks to the boulevards, from the gentle to the angry, from the still to the loud, from the singers to the orators, from the seers to the doers. Once they had forfeited the homage of the eyes, the corpses of words fell onto the dissecting table of the brain: world and language came under the knife. The poem as a weapon, as an object for use, as a means of production. Verses not from the ivory tower, but from the word laboratory. The lyric poet as literary engineer. A process that began with Edgar Allen Poe and Valéry and became with Enzensberger the common property of a generation. Verses more than ever before as a declaration of independence, as provocation, as a declaration of power by the powerless, as indignation and anger. And then, once more, the poem as a sensuous artifact. But sensuousness no longer sighs and is no longer chaste. Neither décolleté nor marble. Sensuousness in the poems of Enzensberger, Grass, Rühmkorf, Biermann whips, whistles, calculates, juggles, flings out lyrical addresses and stirring thrillers. Where the former lyric sought to incorporate the innocence of word and thing, the new lyric tries to prove *a priori* the guilt of others, the guilt of political figures, the guilt of great and small directors, the guilt of cooperators and noncooperators, the guilt of Nazis and of the affluent society, the guilt of authorities, the guilt of programmers, the guilt of all and the innocence of those who write the poems.

Unquestionably, the theme of lyric poetry as well as of the 50s and 60s is man and man's awareness of self and world—at least the awareness of the man who writes verses. Is the one who writes a typical man of his generation? He himself thinks so. And he belongs, in any event, to the alert, to the sensorially gifted, to those who are sensitive to register, perhaps to deform, but nevertheless to reflect threats to and changes in awareness. The writer, including the lyric poet, belongs to those who observe, experience, interpret, communicate the social climate, and give warning of storms to come. Later generations often attempt to prove that the awareness of these men was too little and too late, that their way of thinking was too comfortable, too petty, too unpolitical, or too utopian: thus Heinrich Heine against the aged Goethe, the Young Germans against the Romanticists, the Naturalists against the Classicists and Realists, the Expressionists against the Impressionists, the Nazis against the representatives of "degenerate art." And today after 1945? Since the war, three generations of writers have already made their appearance. The first condemned the Third Reich in the name of the West and of Christianity. The second reproached the first for its "reactionary" Westernism. The most recent are already attacking the generation that belongs to Group 47.

## *A Glance at the Literary Past*

Where literature fails to take cognizance of historical developments, there arise either interpretations that are considered almost absolute because they are immanent in the text, or feuilletonism in the bad sense—well-formulated approbation or indignation without historical perspective. If one is to speak of the individual's awareness of self and world as manifested in German lyric poetry since 1945, it appears proper to consider first an older writer who was, it is true, once modern, but whose work now appears antiquated. I refer to Friedrich Hebbel. In the middle of the nineteenth century, he experienced the fragility of human self-awareness. Although he did not, like a successor of Schiller or a forerunner of Expressionism, want to "embrace the millions," he was nonetheless still able to produce a hymnic portrait of man.

*MAN*
Man—Oh, lofty name! The bliss of heaven is
Poured into your heart by God on high
From out the Sea of Light, from angels' dwelling:
Herein, O man, I find your glory lies.

Lordly, you stepped from the hands of your Creator,
Graced by the Master with the gift to be
Perfect only in immortality;
Graced with the strength to undergo what's hardest:
When right and fancy part, at war, to be
Tossed by passion's waves, in storm at sea.

Man, sacred masterpiece of heaven . . .[1]

Is it chance that this poem, though it has four strophes of ten lines each, has nevertheless remained a fragment? Belief in man's heavenly origin seems to have been preserved. Belief in man's moral activity, in the lofty, in the "stamp" of the "beautiful" and the "perfect" raises its voice once more. In Austria, at the beginning of the twentieth century, Hofmannsthal clung to the ideal of Western, Christian man. Even he had complained in his early *Lebenslied* [Song of Life] (1896) that he was a "homeless heir." Perhaps he could cling to the traditional only because he was not so closely and democratically involved as were the Expressionists in the change and collapse of everything monarchical.

Between Goethe's lines, "Let man be / helpful and good! / For that alone / distinguishes him / from all beings / that we know" (1783), and the "doctor-poems" published in 1917 by Gottfried Benn with the bitter caption, "The crown of creation, the swine, man," a tremendous caesura had taken shape. The caesura that had taken shape and spread was the caesura of Darwin, of Marx, of Helmholtz. It was the doctrine of the complete comprehensibility and constructability of the world, of the organizability of history, and of the responsibility of the many. School rooms were tapestried with

Goethe's poem. But the idealistic imperative was not fulfilled. Undoubtedly, these and similar word-tapestries had their share in lulling the slothful, providing glib phrases for those whose thought processes were feeble, propping up the depleted conscience, and maligning some young agitants who were dissatisfied with so much bourgeois mentality and high-mindedness.

In the Foreword to *Menschheitsdämmerung* (1919), that document of Expressionist lyric that has since become famous, Kurt Pinthus formulated the trend and meaning of the poems, the belief of that generation: "Man as such, not his private concerns and feelings, but humanity, that is the unending theme. These poets were early aware of how man was sinking into the twilight . . . , was sinking into the night of destruction . . . , in order to appear again in the clearing twilight of the past and present that were pressed upon him and that surrounded and engulfed him, in the redeeming twilight of a future that he creates for himself. . . . Whatever in man is not to be scientifically discerned—came here with prophetic truth and clarity into the light. . . . It has become clearer and clearer: man can be saved by man alone."[2] The twilight of man, that means the destruction of the old and the birth of a new man. "The best and most passionate of these writers do not struggle against the outer conditions of mankind, but against the condition of displaced, humiliated, and misled man himself."[3] Their lyrical protest was powerless. Not poems, but potatoes, not volumes of lyrics, but votes made history. Politics, not the more or less refined belief of the lyricists, determined man. The great evil was still not to be found in poetry.

On January 30, 1933 began the twelve years of the "painter" (Hitler). On May 10, 1933, "alien literature" was burned in the public square before the Opera House in Berlin. The assembled students sang: "Born of the people / a Leader has arisen for us, / has given us faith and hope again in Germany. / People, to arms." And Goebbels spoke the grotesquely memorable words: "Here the intellectual basis of the November Republic sinks to the ground; but out of this wreckage will arise the phoenix of a new spirit, a spirit that we will bear, that we will foster, to which we will give a distinctive face and distinctive features."[4] The new man, the blond German beast, was proclaimed and given form. Not ten years later, Nelly Sachs, who had just escaped the murderers, was writing the poems *In den Wohnungen des Todes* [In the Dwellings of Death].

## I. Seven Years of Tradition, Christians, and Returning Soldiers (1945–1952/1953)

### *The Man Who Knows That He Is "Subject to Eternal Laws"*

When the first volumes of lyric poetry began to make their appearance after the war, the best known writers were still in exile: Thomas and Heinrich Mann, Hermann Broch, Alfred Döblin, Anna Seghers, Bertolt Brecht. At first, there was no mention of Brecht, though he is, with Rilke and perhaps Gottfried Benn, the greatest lyric poet of the first half of the century. The first volumes of poetry to appear after the fall of the "painter's" Reich (the word "painter" comes from Brecht) were Werner Bergengruen's *Dies Irae* (1945) and Rudolf Hagelstange's *Venezianisches Credo* [Venetian Credo] (1945 and 1946).[5] They were verses of self-reflection, verses of confrontation with the political power, verses of conscience and judgment, verses that not only belonged formally to tradition, but were actually evolved from an awareness of man that was Western, Christian, and Classical. Both volumes were written during the summer of 1944, at a time when the prophetic glance had very little need of the gift of prophecy.

Bergengruen's lyrical adjurations extend from German Classicism to the Sermon on the Mount, from the prophets' lament over the unrecognized *Epiphany* and the prophesying of *salt and ashes* to the preaching of penance and the call "An die Völker der Erde" [To the Peoples of the Earth] . The epigraph of *Dies Irae* is taken from *Faust II:* "Turn toward clarity / flames of love! / That the self-condemned / May be healed by truth." The last verses of the "cry to the peoples" read:

> O you peoples! the call of judgment applies to us all.
> Together accuse the common betrayal, the common defilement.
> Peoples, hearken with us to the heavenly: Metanoiete![6]

In retrospect, many are of the opinion that this old master of the West with his cry of a Goethe or a Dante, with his prophetic stance, his classical repertoire, and his call to "Metanoiete" was, perhaps, taking the easy path.

Rudolf Hagelstange, a writer who tried to answer for himself toward the end of the war and whose poems became known just after the war, also preceded his poems with a Classical quotation. "It is a fearful thing to be / The mortal vessel of your truth." The quotation is from Schiller's ballad "Kassandra" (1802). Cassandra, the Trojan seeress, sees destruction approaching the walls of her father's city. She begs Apollo to take her "sad clarity" from her. Thus, the lyrical *I* of the *Venezianische Sonette* appears here in the role of a Cassandra. Hagelstange, too, who in the summer of 1945 was a soldier in the German army in northern Italy, pays allegiance to the Western, Classical, Christian "spirit," to the "law" and truth of tradition, to the "likeness of man." For this lyrical *I*, the basic questions about man are of central importance, the answers are unambiguous.

> What does it mean—a man? Are action, speech,
> Enough that we should think ourselves the lords
> Of the world, like Adam, or like Him before
> Adam, who spoke and lo! his creatures each
>
> Opened eyes to life, opened lips to praise.
> What is the weight of the praise, the thanksgiving we offer?
> That utterance has worth which sets our hearts on fire,
> That action, whereby the good the simple obeys.
>
> For a bird can put us to shame, and so too a flower,
> A beetle, a fish, yes, even the stone that lies
> Dark and cold in the stream, that mildly complies
> With each whim of the current's will; and yet do we,
> To summon light from darkness, lack the power,
> To be augmentors of our humanity.[7]

The preceding sonnet inquired of those who have the image and the power: "What did you do? What did you add to the image / of man that it might be unveiled? / . . . Has Michael fallen? Has the image / been lost in the tumult?" Brecht, as his poem *An die*

*Nachgeborenen* reveals, had difficulties with his *Rat der Weisen* [Advice of Wise Men] and *Wort der alten Meister* [Word of the Old Masters]. The experienced Brecht would probably have reacted somewhat as follows to Hagelstange's words: Now, just win "light" from this "darkness" and tell us what that stilted "augmentors of our humanity" is supposed to mean, what it would have done first and concretely to stop a monstrous process of annihilation. But we have no reason here to denigrate the orientation and stance of the younger poet from the standpoint of Brecht's bitter concreteness. In Hagelstange's second volume of poems, *Strom der Zeit* [The Stream of Time] (1948), the formula reads: "a God commands that he [man] find himself again, / and makes him subject to eternal laws."

Bergengruen published his volume of collected poems in 1950 under the title *Die heile Welt* [The Sound World]. Perhaps this older, self-possessed, and innerly self-assured poet could see the world and man in this light. Critics less convinced than he about the world and its soundness ask to what extent Bergengruen and other poets of soundness were aware of the concrete, the detail, the cleavage in man, the helplessness of the political world, and the amorphous quality of society; or to what extent personal faith blankets reality, and the state of being at one with oneself palliates the conflicts of this world; to what extent Western, Christian rhymes still share in the rhymelessness of this world. There is, of course, no question here of anything biographical, but of the introduction into poetry of the world and of the lyrical *I* that has found entry into the world.

One person whose poems were highly autobiographical in nature was Albrecht Haushofer. His *Moabiter Sonette* [Moabit Sonnets] appeared posthumously in 1946. This forty-three-year old professor of geography and geopolitics at the University of Munich belongs to the martyrs of July 20. At the time when Alfred Delp was meditating on his existence in the face of death, Haushofer, in the Lehrter Prison in Berlin, was expressing in sonnets his concept of what it means to be a man. His life was ended shortly before the end of the war by a bullet in the neck. Eastern composure, Christian belief in the resurrection, a sharply political and mystically transcendent awareness mingled in the verses of this widely traveled and cultured scholar. In the thirteenth sonnet, months before the first atom bomb had fallen, he called the Nazis "detonators of nuclear fission rockets." In the fourteenth sonnet, entitled *Qui resurrexit*, Haushofer sought for and found his picture of Christ. The opening line, "I have seen Him in a thousand pictures," is borrowed from Novalis' poem in honor of the Virgin Mary. The diaeresis opens the realm of pictures and aspects. The aspects: "judge of the world," "thorn-crowned," "child of the Madonna." Then the direct application: "Now I feel that only one [picture] is valid: / As he showed Himself to Master Mathis / . . . There, by light surrounded: that is Christ. / . . . Rising weightless from the darkened grave, / . . . In multicolored rays of heavenly light." Haushofer sealed his picture of man and Christ with his martyrdom.

This is not the place to prove in individual detail how, as a group, the women who wrote lyric poetry in the post-war era furthered the traditional and, for the most part, Christian picture of man. In 1946, Marie Luise Kaschnitz published a volume of *Gedichte* [Poems] and Oda Schaefer published her *Irdisches Geleit* [Safe Conduct on Earth]. Christine Lavant published *Die unvollendete Liebe* [The Unconsummated Love] in 1948; Gertrud von Le Fort, *Gedichte* in 1950; Silja Walter, *Gedichte* in 1950; Christine Busta, *Der Regenbaum* [The Raintree] in 1951. The intellectual and emancipated woman, the woman who rigorously questions her grandmother, who takes her place with more or less equal rights and with a strongly intellectual impact in the ruptured world of men with its linguistically harder and more artful tone, does not begin to publish lyric poetry until some years later.

### *Attempts at Orientation by "Returning Soldiers"*

There was a group of lyric poets whose impulse to write sprang from their return home from a lost war into bombed-out cities. They were soldiers. What they wrote was, for a long time, called "coming to terms with the past" or even "lyrics from the rubble." The war and the end of the war had marked their existence. And from time immemorial it has been primarily existence that has found its way into poems. They could not, at least not entirely, turn aside to nature and nature poems, or what are called nature poems.

Wolfgang Weyrauch belonged to this generation, as did Karl Krolow, Hans Egon Holthusen, Günter Eich. Even Paul Celan or Peter Huchel have, each in his own way, a share in it. Marie Luise Kaschnitz and Bertolt Brecht have also, though in different ways, written lyrics about returning soldiers. Today people say that many a returning soldier expressed too much too easily in the poems of those days. But there will always be those who are wise in retrospect. From the formal point of view, some of the least successful poems were those written by Wolfgang Weyrauch. They were published in 1946 by the Aufbau Publishing Company of East Berlin. In his lyric awareness, he was attempting to link "Bruder Rotarmist" [Brother of the Red Army] with the verse from the hymnal, "We are all in God's care"; the Nuremberg Trials with "Dear lady, we are in the cornfield"; "Sleep, my little one, sleep" with a kind of children's crusade against "armored cars." But "ox and ass" and the "American" and the "Russian pilot" were, despite all this lyrical well-meaning, too totally dissimilar to be joined without visible seam in the lyrical coverall of *Von des Glückes Barmherzigkeit* [On the Compassion of Happiness], as the volume was called.

Even Karl Krolow, although more skilled in the use of form, was relatively unsuccessful, especially with his poems on contemporary themes, as for instance, his "Lied, um sein Vaterland zu vergessen" [Song to Forget One's Fatherland], his ode "An den Frieden" [To Peace] (1946), and his "Ode 1950." Krolow's "Lied, um sich seiner Toten zu erinnern" [Song to Remind Oneself of One's Dead] does not appeal to us today. The middle strophes read:

Buried by the enamel heaven
Of sudden death, you're living yet
And from your water flasks you pour
Serenity upon your rest.

The sweet surcease of pain comes lightly,
The guessing games of words have lost
For you their dark obscurity:
The dread that comes to men at night.

Memory, like an egg that's broken,
In you is empty now, serene:

You who greet me have forgotten
Even the rifles you kept so clean.

Be now the stuff of dreams and your own
Image and that other life
Where hands can rest at last in pockets
Idle after all the strife.[8]

"Enamel heaven" and "image"—one's image: what is all that to a dead man? "Serenity" and "dreams," the lyrical "stars," the German "all," and the Western belief in immortality provide a comforting retreat. Let him who can, console himself with such verses. I do not know if anyone has succeeded in doing so. But at the time even Christians understood them as exemplary.

However, there is one successful post-war poem, one authentic poem by and about a soldier, one poem that is a lasting memorial to the dead. Günter Eich's poem "Inventur" [Inventory], written in prison, will have permanent value. Its new, delyricized tone, unpretentious and unpathetical, found no imitators until the 50s.

*Inventory*
This is my cap,
this is my coat,
here are my shaving things
in a linen bag.

These are canned goods:
my plate and my cup.
I've scratched my name
here in the tin.

Scratched it with this
precious nail
that I hide from all
envious eyes.

Here in my haversack
a pair of woolen socks
and some things I'll not
tell anyone about,

so it serves as a pillow
nights for my head.
This cardboard here lies
between me and the earth.

The refills for my pencil
are dearest to me:
by day they write poems
that I compose by night.

This is my notebook,
this my groundsheet,
this is my handkerchief,
this is my thread.[9]

Surely this is a temperate stock-taking. No flight into remembered Classicism, into invocations or preciosity. This lyric *I* does not try to use words to catapult himself out of the banal, the debasing, the comfortless. He takes a stand. He experiences and describes reality.

Perhaps the best poem about returning soldiers was written in exile in 1943 by Bertolt Brecht. For years it was unknown since Brecht, although he had not at first intended to do so, had to return home to East Berlin.

*Return*

My hometown, what will it be like there?
After the swarms of bombers
I come home.

But where's my town? Where the monstrous
Mountains of smoke stand.
There in the flames,
That's it.

My hometown, how will it receive me then?
The bombers were here before me. Deadly swarms
Announce my return. Ravaging flames
Precede the son.[10]

It could hardly be expressed more simply. No tapestries of verses, no demands; it describes reality without pathos, the bombed-out city, the question about it, the question about the poet's own return. "Hometown" and "I" are not talked about, but made present; complaint, uncertainty, perplexity, feeling are all modestly expressed in understatements.

The great laments for the dead also belong to these seven years. The two greatest are by Jewish poets. Both were written outside of Germany. It was some time before either of them became known to German readers. I am referring to"Todesfuge" [The Fugue of Death] by Paul Celan and to Nelly Sachs' cycle of poems about the concentration camps entitled *In den Wohnungen des Todes.* The latter volume was first published in 1946 by the Aufbau Publishing Company in East Berlin, but more than ten years elapsed before it was known and accepted. Toward the German dead, feeling is ambiguous even today. There seem to be no laments for them among the writers of the Federal Republic of (West) Germany except private ones or those filled with empty platitudes. The exception in East Berlin is to be found in the works of Peter Huchel.

## *The Literary Awareness of the Public and the Anthology ERGRIFFENES DASEIN*

Both in content and in language, the poetry that was published and known in the post-war years was dominated by the search for a link with tradition. In the minds of the older writers, the influence of German Classicism was normative. Rilke's influence can be detected everywhere; Expressionism, the tradition of nature poems (Loerke, Lehmann, Langgässer, Britting, and others), sometimes Gottfried Benn and his *Statische Gedichte* [Static Poems] (1948) exert an influence, but not, as yet, Bertolt Brecht. Along with the nature poems, which are not considered here, there was no dearth of poems on contemporary issues. But only a few poets, and fewer still of those who came home from the war and began to write immediately afterwards, evolved a statement of lasting value, a firm lyric form of their own. It is certainly not by accident that the strongest of these poets, Günter Eich and Peter Huchel, had already begun to write in the 30s. On the one hand, the returning soldiers attempted with a speed that is understandable to "come to terms with" the events just past; on the other hand, they took refuge, in their poems, in a new romantic lyricism, in a too quick and too superficial peace. Karl Krolow's "Ode 1950" may be regarded as symptomatic in its lyrical tone, its level of feeling, its sincerely intended opposition to the Existentialists' "talk about nothingness" and their "ghostly mode," in its tendency to reach the "foundation of being" which "is bright and bitter," by means of a "tenderly conceived" lyrical "algebra." Once more, the era and the concrete detail, everything that did or should move souls, were avoided. Once more, the "foundation of being" was adjured in an Old German and "mystic" manner and savored in an attitude of wisdom. Here the sublime was the substitute. In other poems, as, for instance, in those of Wolfgang Weyrauch, where the leap was hazarded to a concrete, contemporary awareness, the attempt was unsuccessful on the linguistic level. In 1953, Rudolf Hagelstange's *Ballade vom verschütteten Leben* [Ballad of the Buried Life] afforded a significant last example of the traditional narrative poem on a contemporary issue. It was a realistic depiction of the six years at the end of the war during which German soldiers were buried in a reserve air-raid shelter in Gdingen.

The lyrical awareness of those years is reflected in the anthology *Ergriffenes Dasein* [Entranced Existence] (Ebenhausen: Munich, first edition, 1953) with its Afterword by Hans Egon Holthusen and Friedrich Kemp. The fact that the link with tradition has been found and seems to have been everywhere preserved evokes evident satisfaction. Werner Bergengruen, Karl Krolow, the Schnack brothers, Georg von der Vring, and Hans Egon Holthusen are represented in this anthology, some with just as many poems as, and some with more poems than Bertolt Brecht. Paul Celan, whose "Todesfuge" had been published in the preceding year, and Nelly Sachs, whose second volume of poems had appeared in 1949, were not represented. Nor was Günter Eich's "Inventur" included. The German lyric tradition had indeed been preserved. Peace seemed to have descended upon the pool of German lyric poetry with its mother-of-pearl tones and its surrounding roses, classical busts, and statues of Ophelia. Peace and nothing new and no literary complaints about existence. Formulas like *Bewahrung und Gewinn in der Dichtung aus christlichem Geist* [Conservation and Gain in the Literature from the Christian Spirit]—written in 1953 with a pen honed on Christianity—can hardly be regarded today from a point of view so unambiguously positive and so laden with self-sanction as was then intended.[11] The world was not so "sound" as many believed it to be. The refound tradition, as it was called, whether classical, Christian, or of some other variety, revealed, upon closer scrutiny, appalling deficiencies in thought, perception, and text. Its truth, to quote Brecht, was not concrete enough. At the time, that was obviously not noted in the ranks of the "West," in the broad sense of the term. Today, it is evident. Its truth, to quote Brecht, was not concrete enough. The present could not be satisfactorily shaped and described by a mere evocation of the past.

## II. The New Generation or the Thirteen Years of Group 47 (1952/1953–1965/1966)

Not everyone in the post-war years was reassured by the newly found link with tradition. At first, the non-reassured were still to be found in the ranks of returning soldiers. They differed from those who were satisfied not so much in age as by reason of their more radically changed awareness. They no longer believed that patterns of thought and behavior could so easily be assimilated from the past. They were no longer ready to work docilely to win the inheritance of their fathers. They were convinced that their fermenting spirit had to find new ways and forms. Since they found few models already in existence and ready for use, they needed more time to express themselves. They insisted on their own creative way. Collectively, they became known as "Group 47." The name originated at the time of the suppression of the journal *Der Ruf* [The Summons], but was not used publicly until the 50s as a designation for the group that was influencing the whole literary life of the Federal Republic (of West Germany).[12] Several years were to pass before the Group held a meeting or read their works publicly. Both events occurred in 1952–1953. At the meeting in May 1952 in Niendorf on the Baltic Sea, the older members of the Group read first from the manuscripts of their novels. Walter Jens reports: "And then, suddenly, it happened. A man by the name of Paul Celan (no one had heard the name before) began . . . to read his poems; Ingeborg Bachmann, a debutante, whispered some verses in a hesitant and husky voice; Ilse Aichinger read aloud . . . her "Spiegelgeschichte" [Mirror Story]. At that meeting, seven years after the end of the war, was born . . . the young German literature of the contemporary era."[13]

### *The Revolutionary Years of the Lyric*

Paul Celan's first volume of poetry, *Mohn und Gedächtnis* [Poppy and Memory], appeared as early as 1952 (seventh edition, 1965). It contained the famous "Todesfuge." Walter Höllerer, later one of the best critics in Group 47, published his volume of poems, *Der andere Gast* [The Other Guest], in 1952. In 1953, Ingeborg Bachmann, who wrote her doctoral dissertation on Heidegger, brought out a volume to which she gave the title *Die gestundete Zeit* [Borrowed Time]. Helmut Heissenbüttel, who later joined Group 47, wrote "Einfache Sätze" [Simple Sentences]. The Swiss German, Eugen Gomringer, who was born in Bolivia and worked for several years with Max Bill in the School of Design in Ulm, withstood the attraction of the group; in 1953, he brought out the most concrete textual effort that had yet appeared, his *konstellationen* [constellations]. *Akzente* [Accents], the literary journal of the young generation, began to appear in 1954. Walter Höllerer and Hans Bender edited it in Munich. It was not the journal of the Group, but many of the Group worked on it and there developed, in consequence, a strong communication between the journal and the Group. Broad literary contacts with Anglo-American and French literature became evident (a decade later, intensive efforts were made to become acquainted with and to translate the literature of Communist countries). It was also in 1954 that Heissenbüttel published his volume of poetry entitled *Kombinationen* [Combinations]. In 1955, Celan published his second volume, *Von Schwelle zu Schwelle* [From Threshold to Threshold]. In the same year, Hans Bender edited the volume *Mein Gedicht ist mein Messer* [My Poem Is My Knife], which was effective in bringing about changes in lyric poetry and which later appeared in a pocket edition. With the volume *Die Vorzüge der Windhühner* [The Advantages of Wind Hens], Günter Grass entered the arena in 1956. Ingeborg Bachmann presented her second volume of lyrics, *Anrufung des Grossen Bären* [Invocation of the Big Dipper]. In the same year, Walter Höllerer edited the anthology *Transit. Lyrikbuch der Jahrhundertwende* [Transit. Book of Mid-Century Lyrics], which was characteristic for these years of transition. It attempted to show the present not as the retention of the old, but as an upsurge of the new, to make visible something like an avant-garde of the lyric. Hans Magnus Enzensberger, who had made his debut in *Akzente*, was also represented in *Transit*. In the following year, 1957, Enzensberger trumpeted his *verteidigung der wölfe* [Defense of the Wolves] provocatively across the land. Together with Werner Riegel, Peter Rühmkorf, who was already being discussed in 1956, brought out *Heisse Lyrik* [Hot Lyric], a West German variant of the beat lyric in the United States. Rühmkorf, who had never been a soldier, also joined Group 47. In 1959, and quite apart from the group, Franz Mon published his economically written *artikulationen* [articulations]. Rühmkorf, in the same year, paraded and parodied with his *Irdisches Vergnügen in g* [Earthly Happiness in *g*]. In 1959 and 1960, Nelly Sachs received her first honors from German sources. Her lyrics, which are not only unmodish, but also unmodern, belong to none of the literary groups with their formal distinctions. But she was discovered—that must be said—by members of Group 47. In 1960, Enzensberger cast his *landessprache* [vernacular] onto the lyric market. In the same year, he compiled his *Museum der modernen Poesie* [Museum of Modern Poetry]. It contains poems in sixteen languages from the years 1910–1945, both in the original and in translation. The volume is introduced by the important Foreword on the "Weltsprache der modernen Poesie" [World Langauge of Modern Poetry].[14] Recent German lyric poetry had had its look at the world and had found its own orientation. At the price of increasing uniformity, it was in the process of leaving provincialism behind. In the virtuosity with which linguistic elements were utilized, in the politically aggressive tone, in the demand for freedom and demythologizing, in the sentimental search for a Jazz arcadia, it had come into its own.

Since about 1965 or 1966, there have been clear indications that Group 47, as a group that appeared after the war and bore the marks of both war and postwar years, is gradually disintegrating.

### *Enzensberger and the Attack on Society*

Paul Celan's verbal artistry is built on a surrealistic foundation and a striving for greater and greater economy of expression; despite innumerable printings, his works remain, so far as society is concerned, on the periphery, perhaps because they embody a lyric that is not only astringent and hard to understand, but also nonpolitical and relatively unattractive to the public. Ingeborg Bachmann retained the elemental sensitivity to life that distinguished her both as an Austrian and as a woman. For all her modern alertness, for all her solicitude for time borrowed and to be brought to fruition, she persisted imperturbably in her use of the old-fashioned word "love" and did not let herself be falsely diverted either by "sex" or by the activities of artists and minstrels.[15] The works of Franz Mon and Eugen Gomringer did not attract a wide circle of readers. Heissenbüttel spells, associates, abstracts, forces grammar attentively through a textual brain. These text exercises are very wearisome. The reproduction of images, quotations, montages of texts, abstractions becomes the critical demonstration of a consciousness that is uncritical toward history, modes of behavior, use of language, information. The vernacular, as it were, applied to textual patterns. Günter Grass's poetry is as vivid, as fluent, as rich in images as his prose. In his workshop-castle, his play instinct and his sense of commitment have found a hiding-place that is by turns lighthearted, playfully shrewd, exasperated, and belligerent, and where there are play corners and pleasure courts, sulking benches and badminton, protest towers next to hen-houses, and podia for scolding and objective dispute.[16]

Social criticism and a nonconformist mode of speech permeate nearly all of today's poetry. In today's literary market, they are the equivalent of what used to be called the "eternal laws." Enzensberger stands at the exact center of the poetry of social criticism and of the young generation. His poems put the affluent society on trial. Something of the anger of the American "beat generation"[17] and of Brecht's manner pulses in his veins, although it must be admitted that he lacks the genius of Brecht's minstrelsy and his (at least at that time) Marxist conviction, as well as the tremendous human and creative tension that arises from both of these—from the minstrel-like artistry and the claims of dogmatic Marxism. Enzensberger's poem, "ins lesebuch für die oberstufe" [for a senior-class reader], is reminiscent both of Brecht's lyrical "Lesebuch für Städtebewohner" [Reader for Citydwellers] and of the poem "Die Antwort" [The Answer]: "My young son asks me: Should I study mathematics?"[18] Enzensberger makes it very obvious that man can no longer regard himself idealistically as an individual or as an individually vain image of God, contented with the universe and unresponsive to the rest of mankind. Evident in these poems are the manifold contingencies of the individual and the fluctuating relationship between man and society; the prevenient definition of man, which no longer represents him as the image of God and which displaces the concept of the concrete; an alert attentiveness to time as present time, as that for which man must render an account and which he is to shape democratically.

*for a senior-class reader*
don't read odes, my son, read timetables:
they're more exact. unroll the sea charts
before it is too late. be vigilant, don't sing.
the day is coming when they will again paste lists
upon the door and brand their mark onto the breasts
of dissenters. learn to go incognito, learn more than I did:
change your quarters, your passport, your face.
learn to perform the small treachery,
the daily mean evasion. encyclicals
are good for lighting fires,
manifestos for wrapping butter and salt
for the defenseless, anger and endurance are needed
to blow into the lungs of power
the deadly powder finely ground
by those who have learned much,
who are exact, by you (V 85).[19]

The orientation of Enzensberger's poems is social. They seek to recognize, to warn, to challenge to action and to resistance. They provoke and attack.

*defense of the wolves against the lambs*
should the vulture feed on forget-me-nots?
do you expect the jackal
to shed his skin? the wolf
to pull out his own teeth?
what do you dislike
about commissars and popes?
why do you stare stupidly from your shirts
at the lying screen?

who sews the blood-red stripe on the
general's trousers? who
carves the capon for the usurer?
who proudly hangs the tin cross
over his rumbling navel? who
takes the tip, the piece of silver,
the hush money? there are
many who are robbed, but few who are thieves;
who applauds them, then, who
wears the insignia, who
thirsts for the lie?

look in the mirror: cowards,
shunning the effort of the truth,
averse to learning, leaving
thought to the wolves,
a nose-ring your most precious jewel,
no deceit too stupid, no solace
too cheap, every blackmail
is still too mild for you.

you lambs, compared to you
crows are sisters:
you blind each other.
fraternity rules
among the wolves:
they hunt in packs.

praised be the robbers: you
inviting rape,
throw yourselves upon the indolent bed
of obedience, whimpering,
yet still you lie. you want
to be torn to pieces. you'll
not change the world (V 9) f.).[20]

This unusual defense is a modern version of the old fables. That means, it is a didactic poem. It speaks of two kinds of men: wolves and lambs. Both, of course, are treated with irony. At first it is said of the wolves merely that they are wolves and do not plan to change their nature. Examples of wolf-like individuals are mentioned: "commissars and popes," the "general" and the "usurer." The arrangement conceals a rhetorical trick. When two unlike and widely separated objects are juxtaposed, it creates tension. The juxtaposition hangs the objects like puppets from a wire: behold the villains. And who joins them? Who shares their activity? Who approves the wolves? Answer: whoever "takes the tip, the silver piece, the hush money," whoever "thirsts for the lie." The one who takes a tip in imagined innocence, the one who puts himself at the disposal of others, is unaware of this. His conscience must first be awakened. In the first strophe, the lyric speaker points out the wolves to the lambs. From strophe to strophe, he shows the lambs their expendability, holds up the mirror before their faces—recognize yourselves: "cowards, / shunning the effort of the truth, / averse to learning, leaving / thought to the wolves," and so on. You are the lambs, but ". . . compared to you / crows are sisters: / you blind each other." There is no trace of community, of "fraternity." You could learn from the wolves, for "they hunt in packs."

The final strophe offers provocative praise of the wolves. For ". . . you / inviting rape, / throw yourselves upon the indolent bed / of obedience, whimpering, / yet still you lie. you want / to be torn to pieces. you'll / not change the world." The defense of the wolves is intended with just as much irony as the designation "lambs" for the cowardly, for those who are too lazy to think, for the slothful who fall into the role of "obedience" and deceive themselves and the world that they are innocent and defenseless. There is no mention here of the man who is alert and self-critical. Though they are passive among themselves, the lambs are ready and quite able to tear one another's eyes out. Men of this caliber have only negative qualities in common with lambs. This pseudo-lamb nature has to be exposed and attacked. Line for line in this *defense of the wolves,* man's image and his understanding of himself are being questioned. The reader is supposed to recognize the wolves, his own role as a slothful and cowardly lamb, and his share in the domination of the wolves. The poem calls for men who are critical toward the world and toward themselves, who recognize the "robbers" and their own false nature as lambs, who arm themselves against the wolves and establish communication with a society of their own kind. The poem is a challenge to man to recognize himself and to act accordingly. It is an eminently political poem, a challenge to the man who is just a fellow-traveler.

These are verses that Brecht might have written, but not Benn. Benn did not believe that the lyric poet could or should become involved in the bustle of the world.[21] Brecht, on the other hand, was convinced that the poet has an obligation to help change the world. Enzensberger reveals himself as the disciple of Brecht. Benn's lyrics were primarily contemplative. Those of Brecht and Enzensberger have a positive intention. Benn's lyric *I*, when it felt that it had been offended, withdrew from society and became individualistic. Like Brecht, Enzensberger consciously confronts society, attacks it, holds up the mirror before its face, seeks to teach it. Benn was primarily interested in producing beautiful poetry; in the midst of treachery and futility, he wanted to be sure of form as of an absolute. Like Brecht, Enzensberger wanted to write utilitarian lyrics, not structures that were isolated from life, but comprehensible and useful poems that served life.[22]

In his second volume, *landessprache* [vernacular], Enzensberger makes an even stronger attack on the wolves and the lambs, the greedy, the uncritical, the amorphous in the affluent society of West Germany. He unmasked their language, its current catchwords, its key words, the lyrical and cultural quotations that were again popular, the language of all who, in their wolves' and lambs' skins, were interested only in "improving the standard of living" as quickly, efficiently, and smoothly as possible, that is, without any human considerations.

*vernacular*

. . . . . . . . . . . . . . . . . . . . . . . . .
things are going upwards here
it's good to be here,
where it goes upwards backwards,
here the leading gentleman shoots down the leading gentleman
with the hymnbook,
here the lightly wounded wage war
against the badly wounded,
here the rule is: be inexorably nice to each other,
. . . . . . . . . . . . . . . . . . . . . . . . . . . . . . . . . . . . . . . .
here let us build tabernacles
on this heap of Aryan scrap-metal
on this cacophonous parking lot
where ruins spring from ruins,
brand new, ruins in stock, on instalment
on call, on recall:

to be here is wonderful,
. . . . . . . . . . . . . . . . . . . .
in this den of murderers,
where the calendar tears off its pages in impotence and haste,
where the past smoulders in the refuse disposals
and the future grinds its false teeth,
that's because things are going upwards,
then we put stain remover on it,
that's quite customary here, it doesn't surprise me.
we do things right here,
where the positive leads the market,
the chambers of commerce lay in a store of it
and display it under bullet-proof glass,
where we find ourselves among blind men,
in mortuaries, warehouses, and museums.
. . . . . . . . . . . . . . . . . . . . . . . . . . . . . . . . . . .
what have I lost here, why do I poke
and search in this inappropriate tangle
of decorations for hand-to-hand combat, pleasure coupons,
chamois beards, bargain sales, and find nothing

but chronic, chronological gyms
and official experts of humaneness
in the barracks for the barracks for the barracks:

what am I supposed to do here? to say
in what language? and to whom?
. . . . . . . . . . . . . . . . . . . . . . . . . . .
germany, my land, unholy heart of the nations,
rather discredited from defeat to defeat
. . . . . . . . . . . . . . . . . . . . . . . .(L 7–13).[23]

That sounds angry, ill-tempered, aggressive. But no one will be able to say that it avoids the issue, that it speaks in whispers or in ciphers, that it erects a lyrical cuckoo's nest in the clouds. These lines examine, ascertain, take a stand, often exaggerate, simplify, distort, but nevertheless they indicate clearly the reality that has been exploited and turned into a cliché by both wolves and lambs. They speak in the vernacular, in the language of those who go to church and to the movies, the language of the "partners in a wage contract" or of those poisoned by greed, the language of the forgetful and the "superficial." They unmask some of the clichés and quotations commonly used by those who pose as merchants of culture. They make no appeal to the idealistic imperative with "Let man be noble, / helpful and good"; nor do they smudge their business sense by pasting on references to man-in-the-image-of-God. What could be more true than the fact that we were, and have been for some years, the "unholy heart of the nations"? Hölderlin and we, "we have nothing in common." Or would someone venture seriously to maintain that Hölderlin's ecstasy about what is holy has anything in common with our asphalt thinking? Generations of readers have soothed themselves with classical poetry, tasted the beautiful, and risen to dizzying heights on the sublime. Enzensberger disturbs, disillusions, drags the sublime before the very unsublime instincts. In his verses, as well as in his critical essays, there takes place within our circumscribed living space, a new inventory of the human and the less human. There takes place a new poetic *landnahme* [taking of the land], as the title of one of his poems reads:

my land, I do not spare you,
mortal myself, I hold you up
to this mortal light (L 75).[24]

## *Man as "Anti-Icarus" in Rühmkorf's Works*

For a decade now, Peter Rühmkorf has been conveying a very strong rejection of the concept of man as made in the image of God, of the Christian or classical image of man. His "no" comes in a minstrel tone, light-footed, and sentimental, as something close to total parody. Sentimental in a twofold sense: as an intellectual form of writing that is modern in its awareness of crises (this is Schiller's meaning of the word "sentimental"), but also as a projection of sentiment, of a fall and winter carnival of feeling divorced from spirit. It is well-known that parody is a frequently used form in contemporary literature. Where the poet once made use of nature motifs, he turns today to collections of quotations. Quotations afford a double advantage. For one thing, they already possess tension of form: as statements already formed, they are materials raised to the second power. In addition, they permit alienation and deformation. The writer of parody not only exhibits his cultural diploma. As an enlightened man and a new romantic, he uses parody to treat with indifference centuries, continents, creeds. The writer who experiences his powerlessness in this technical world (and who often adverts to it) can give his Pegasus the rein of parody and in lordly freedom take intoxicated possession of the world. The parodist as minstrel also plays the role of king. Today's minstrels do not beg—they demand. Rühmkorf parodies from Homer to Matthias Claudius, from Oswald von Wolkenstein to Benn; he parodies Klopstock and Hölderlin, Greek myths and the Merseburg Charms. What the cross is to the devil, the sublime seems to be to Rühmkorf. He cannot abide it, cannot let it retain value even where it is historically in place. The verse temples of the centuries are the sources and quarries of his ridicule, useful only for lighting fireworks of parody. From the standpoint of form, Rühmkorf's teacher is Gottfried Benn.

In a century that is post and anti-idealistic, the Icarus theme first appears in the works of Benn. As a young man in 1913, he wrote in *Gesänge* [Songs]:

> There fell Icarus at our feet,
> cried: commit fornication, children!
> Straight into the badly-aired Thermopylae!
> Then tossed us one of his shin bones,
> Fell down, was dead.[25]

In Schickele's *Die Weissen Blätter*, two years later (1915), Benn published an Icarus poem in three parts. The *I*, which is deeply but only lately aware, pleads with "noon" to be "unbrained"; the individual split between "animal" and "brain" pleads with "wide-vaulted" noon for just an hour's surcease from this tense and lonely cleavage, for oneness [even if it means] the "melting away of its temples" and the "drinking of its deforeheaded blood." This is still Icarus, admittedly one "screaming himself to pieces with curses in the nothingness," but still one who was guided by the sun, who longed for its liberating and redeeming light.[26] Later, disappointed and embittered by experience, Benn wrote "Verlorenes Ich" [Lost Ego] (1943), a poem whose mood permeates his whole work like a leitmotif:

> Man, battles of nations, Catalonian Plains
> down the beast's gullet.
>
> The world thought to pieces. And space and times
> and all that mankind wove and weighed,
> now just functions of infinities–
> the myth lied.[27]

Rühmkorf says in the poem entitled "Anti-Ikarus": "Myth kapuuut. The moths in Wieland's shirt. / Laica, the lovely, rots in considerable death."[28] And in "Sentimentalisch I":

> Open the bulkheads, boom of consciousness
> —a quite late-bloomer—
> you lift your head full of antiquity
> and lap clean heaven's bowls.
> . . . . . . . . . . . . . . . . . . . . . . . .

Not you, you're not chosen,
so you go empty—and you'd been thinking
the dandruff scales on your head were all numbered
my son, my lost son
. . . . . . . . . . . . . . . . .
Figures pissed into the sand,
Lenin and Winnetou . . .

Of what moment in history,
Alas, of what day are you the offspring–?–
You'll always be just the one who cadges morsels
in the putrid rot of existence.[29]

Rühmkorf's teacher, Benn, was still lamenting the lost salvation, the lost "center," the longing for silent communion with the One Who is not isolated, Who transcends time. "Through every hour, / through every word / the wound of creation / continues to bleed." Benn still sings the lament of creation and, even in his lamenting "no," testifies to the sudden brightening of creation.[30] In his own way, that is, by means of form, Benn tended toward the sublime. Rühmkorf's "Selbstporträt 1958" [Self-Portrait 1958] would never have occurred to Benn. It begins:

How fine to have understood nothing and yet
to enjoy a noseful of mortality–:
the stout son of a moment,
sauntering now among many enemies and few brothers,
taught by sad experience and
thoroughly distrustful of the earth from which he
fancies he was made . . .

he trots, devoid of every higher goal
trip-trop trip-trop,
an asthenic wolf in orange glow,
. . . . . . . . . . . . . . . . . . . . . . . . . . . .
licking his coat smooth, his strained structures,
when he frees himself thoughtfully from syrupy embraces–

The Song of Songs of disobedience–
barked or proclaimed–
but no one has ever done it as meaningfully
as he (I 23).[31]

Rühmkorf's "wolf" and his summons to "disobedience" are different from those of Enzensberger. For Enzensberger affirms society, especially when he attacks it. Rühmkorf portrays himself as the "asthenic wolf," as a being that draws man and things to itself, that knows no limit but his own lack of greater strength. In another place, he calls himself the "wolf in sheep's clothing" (I 17). His summons to "disobedience" is that of the minstrel, of the new Bohemian; it is all-embracing. This *I* gives itself airs, writes in lyrical capitals: "BUT I ATTEST TO NOTHING! / I REFLECT EVERYTHING! "[32] Reflection coined into verses serves as a justification for not having to bear witness. Rühmkorf's "Nichts" [nothing] has little in common with Benn's. It is a minstrel's nothing, totally individualistic; it begins and ends with a pleasurable *carpe diem*, with wine, woman, and song.

Nonetheless, Rühmkorf does bear witness to something, and, in fact, quite programatically: "No transcendence, no gods, no false bottoms. With rampant soul and honest intellect: 'trusting in the *principium individuationis* or in the manner in which the individual knows things: as appearances' " (I 34). Rühmkorf bears witness against that which Christians call heaven and against the exalted demand that the Greeks and the classicists symbolized in the figure of Icarus. Rühmkorf declares: "heaven with the fat skimmed off" (I 6), "the world experienced in one's own fall" (I 7), "as a fallen angel - good! - / enjoy yourself: / Peace after the fall / . . . enjoy the suppleness of your knees; / independent / skin and skum of a perverted spring, / as it made its way to sweet ruin: / Nothing to keep!" (I 17). Rühmkorf had the bad taste to add the following strophe to his parody of Klopstock's ode *Der Zürchersee* [Lake Zurich]:

We're here, comrades, that's irrefutable
—if nothing proves it to us but the flesh that's warm inside our pants—
mortal man stammers all the louder:
Coeo ergo sum! (I 32).

In another place, the "fallen angel" is called "Anti-Icarus":

I spring from the dust, yes indeed, from the earth, I spring
from the stones,
no more condors in the brainy hurst–!

Who comes to weep for the rise and fall
of the winged ape when he transmits fear in morse code
into the air? (I 37).[33]

Is Rühmkorf's "fallen angel" blasphemous—or does he exist "in the circle of the animal kingdom" (I 24) only because man has so determined? The assertion that man is a "winged ape" who "transmits fear in morse code into the air," or that man is a "chained Icarid" (I 37) still seems to point upwards. For this asthenic Shelley, if I may be permitted the expression, who beats out verses on every refuse heap, cannot, as "ape," forget his wings and his "heaven" (cf. I 33). Perhaps the insolent minstrel tone that clings to "what can be grasped" (I 28) only partially conceals a suppressed longing and a fear of death.

Rühmkorf's earthly songs celebrate Western decadence, the decadence of the large city. The rebukes of the minstrel and a kind of pop-longing, self-irony and an intentional destruction of every claim to the sublime, sentimentally clown-like play and the satire of the cabaret—all these urge "Anti-Icarus" to his "Zamek-soup," to the reality that he can experience and enjoy, to the presentation of an express experience of the nonabsolute ("I will turn out no absolute thing"), to "Vodka," wife-song-play, and spite. Rühmkorf has relayed the "why," the "how," and the "where" of his lyric mode of speaking in his "Anleitung zum Widerspruch" [Primer of Contradiction]:

> Tradition superseded, permanence not to be assured, validity questioned, that, it seemed to him, had to be stated explicitly, that had to be established first, and only after the "over and done with," only after the declaration that these things had been rejected, could the possibility of art begin again, if it ever could begin. Of an art distinguished by no anointing, but captivated by unbelief, of an art that could, perhaps, no longer be a poem, but that might be, nonetheless, a "poem," poem in parentheses, parody: a pure case of contradiction: a combined song-for-the-time-being and a song-in-spite-of-everything.[34]

## *Attempt at Criticism and Comparison*

Rühmkorf and Enzensberger represent the two most extreme poles among the lyric poets of a generation. Both are critics in their verses. Both have, in different ways, places where their awareness is weak.

Enzensberger divided the world into three realms: an administered world (example: the Federal Republic of West Germany), a still natural Arcadia (example: the Greek Mediterranean region in the south and the Scandinavian countries in the north), and a "utopia," a dreamland that exists nowhere. The administered world is rejected as being deceptive and hostile to life. The natural world is praised for its simplicity and its lack of dissimulation. "Utopia," obviously, would be the paradisiac happiness of dreams. As a critic, Enzensberger overlooks the fact that, at least in our area and era, the industrial and the Arcadian world, the highly industrialized and the early agrarian individual, are mutually exclusive. He overlooks the fact that people in the land of his "Macedonian shepherd" (V 12 f.) have not even looked closely at some of the social and culturo-political questions that people here have already solved or, at least, begun to solve. He overlooks the fact that the Middle-European simply cannot pass his life in "Greenland," "Iceland," or "Lapland." Such an Arcadia and such pristine stillness do not present the industrial man with a viable alternative. It may be acceptable as a lament for a lost harmony and stillness (Schiller's elegy), but it is sadly inadequate as an answer to a complaint as sharp and one-sided as Enzensberger's against our present situation, if only because our living space cannot be regarded as purely negative, nor can the Arcadia that he envisages be regarded as purely positive, or as a real alternative or a realizable present. And, finally, Enzensberger's dream of "utopia," which repeatedly, both implicitly and explicitly, permeates the early poems, is hardly capable of defending itself against the criticial ideas of an adult individual. In the poems of the third volume, *blindenschrift* [braille] (1964), Enzensberger has withdrawn his anger and ranting indignation at the wickedness of others. His black-white manner has been replaced by tones of gray, "shadow work," signs of the poet's patience and even resignation toward the political sphere. His discernment is no longer heaped lopsidedly onto his rhetoric.

A lyric poet of East Berlin has introduced the criticism of Rühmkorf into the annals of literature. He is Günter Kunert, born like Rühmkorf in 1929. To the verses of Rühmkorf, the minstrel who has lost or given up his goal, to the Western motif of *carpe diem*, Kunert opposes his own verses:

He who decides to live
Must know
Why he awakened yesterday in the night
Where he is going today through the streets
To what end tomorrow he will whitewash
The walls of his room.

Was there a cry?
Is there a goal?
Will there be safety?[35]

Kunert calls this poem "Sorgen" [Cares].[36] On the next page of the same volume, *Verkündigung des Wetters* [Weather Forecast], is to be found his counter-poem to Rühmkorf's "Anti-Ikarus." It reads:

*Icarus 64*

1
Flying is hard:
Both hands stick to the lever of machines:
In need of money.
Feet are glued
To the gas pedal and the dance floor. The head
Is firmly riveted into the proud, progressive
prejudice-hard
Crash helmet.

2
Ballast: The tepid spare-rib
In the family crypt of the stomach.
Ballast: The dark blood
Congested in a prominent place
Near the belt.
Tones
Of the first, second, ninth, thirtieth symphony
Piled ear-high as cultural overweight.
Squandered past
Packed in wieldy urns.
Tanksful of nondisposable tears in stock:
Flying is hard.

3
Nevertheless, spread your arms out and take
A leap at the impossible.
Take a running leap so that you
Fly away
To your heaven
Where all the stars are dimming out.

4
For the day is coming
A horizon is always visible.
Take a leap.[37]

Those are verses with no rhetorical flourish, no parody of decadent irritability. In East Berlin in 1964, it would appear, Icarus was still a possibility as an exemplary figure that seems to be both conceivable and meaningful. In East Berlin, a man says, "nevertheless. . . ." Here in the West, where freedom is bought at a lower price, where people are throwing the last taboos into the rubbish, where one man, in public address, deduces his proof of existence from *coitus* (Rühmkorf, I 32), the self-conscious lyric ego thinks itself enlightened and heroic if it formulates its program with the freedom of the minstrel, "suspend yourself in gravity" (I 6). Was Rühmkorf sufficiently aware that he was rhyming a placeless groan with new Bohemian *(Stöhnen/Neu-Böhmen)*, that, as co-possessor of a common consciousness that has historically displayed little differentiation, he exploits the process of demythologizing as a quarry for his own production?

According to Benn, the problem is this: What does a poet do, in this country (West Germany), when he has long ago stopped believing in what is called Western and lofty; does not have Brecht's and Enzensberger's faith in the political; and has equally little faith in an artistic absolute that, in Benn's meaning of the word, overcomes nothingness with form? A possible answer is that afforded by *Irdisches Vergnügen in g*. The poet less as a fool (the fool nourishes himself on existence) than as a minstrel of the boulevards, as a "Baal" in a lower key. Brecht had noted that Baal ends pleasurably and logically in "nothingness," that Baal can be only a youthful period and an anarchical, vital, basic feeling. Rühmkorf's "Anti-Icarus" is no more able than Brecht's Baal to do justice to this reality. Like Baal, Anti-Icarus is, despite his criticism of society and of consciousness, an egocentric narcissist. Since 1962, Rühmkorf has published no more volumes. As a poet, apparently, he could make no further progress in this direction and mood.

In a way different from that of Helmut Heissenbüttel and his *Texts*, it seems to me, Rühmkorf and Enzensberger are only partially alert to the dangers inherent in man's situation and to the defects in our society. Their awareness of their age is one-sided, eclectic, truncated. The call of the lyric poet for information, clarification, social criticism, linguistic criticism, demythologization has meaning only so long as he is aware of his own partial nature and does not advance with the claim of a new totality, a new Gospel, that only too soon reveals its cloven hoof, its limping pseudo-ideological content. At the same time, however, it is well to recall that not just the lyric, but all literature that lays claim to totality has been problematical for some generations now.

Where they have not overlooked the vertical dimension of human existence, the *homo religiosus*, the lyric poets whom we have thus far been discussing have either disavowed it or accorded it the supercilious smile of a late Enlightenment. They fail to say, or they say only partially, what man is and is not, what he wants and does not want.

Nelly Sachs is a lyric poetess who knows the full dimension of the vertical, who sees man as a creature and raises his battered image aloft to God. Tried by suffering, filtered through death, purified by the faith of her fathers, she sees man's deep "wound" of development in this age. She inquires, for instance, as a purely sociological and political claim to truth:

> If the prophets broke in
> through the doors of night
> tearing wounds with their words
> into the fields of habit,
> bringing something from afar
> for the laborer
> who no longer waits at evening—
>
> If the prophets broke in
> through the doors of night
> and sought an ear like a homeland—

Ear of man
overgrown with nettles,
would you hear?
. . . . . . . . . . . . . .
If the prophets rose up
in the night of mankind
like lovers seeking the heart of the beloved,
night of mankind
would you have a heart to give?[38]

Contemporary lyric offers not only social criticism, demythologizing, and parody in its consideration of man, it offers also the prophetic ear. It depicts not only the technically skilled forms of horizontal demasking and distortion, not only the lewd parodies of a minstrel's no man's land, but also toiling and immortal man. Contemporary man is far removed from Rilke's message, "To be here is glorious," and from his later position, "Nowhere, beloved, will there be world, but within us" *(Seventh Duiner Elegy)*. Not only the world, which is almost totally transformed for the man of this age, but even his completely different awareness (some poets know this) offers a considerable hazard to man's balance. But man, including the man who speaks and portrays himself lyrically, is nevertheless quite prepared—and this applies even to those authors who protest—to meet the challenges of being a man in this world, to meddle in this world boldly and courageously with his democratic weakness. "My great big yes builds sentences with small no's," Günter Grass wrote at the head of a series of poems in his latest volume *Ausgefragt* [Interrogated] (1967). This epigraph may be regarded as both formal and symptomatic.

### *The New Caesura: Poems of Protest and Distrust*

Under various guises and in various tones (often enough in an exalted or parodistic tone, in a tone that was aggressively unencoded or confusedly hermetic), the reader of poetry in the 50s and 60s encountered over and over again the venerable flying-suit so beloved of an older generation (Nelly Sachs, Rühmkorf, Kunert, Paul Celan) and the even more venerable shroud (Kaschnitz, Heissenbüttel, Nelly Sachs). In an age that proceeds philosophically and culturally "without a guiding image" (Adorno), that tends toward the nonrepresentational and still accepts as "representation" only photographs or structural models, the "representation" of man has also become difficult from a literary and lyrical point of view. The question about man and about the society that makes man man has not been silenced; it is to be found in angry and parodistic tones, in verses written in shirtsleeves and trousers.

In 1965–1966, a new caesura becomes apparent, not only in Group 47, which bears the marks of its approaching dissolution, but also in the production of poetry generally. It is not so great as the caesura of 1950, when the writers of Group 47 replaced the "Westerners," the watchmen and heralds of the "loss of the center," as literary leaders. But it is unmistakable: in the generations, in the increasing unrest in regard to the former cultural society and the well-established affluent society, in the poems of protest. Since the "Zurich Literary Dissension" (Dec. 17, 1966) and the continuing debate that it engendered about the end of bourgeois criticism, the caesura has also become evident in the field of criticism.

For some years, the new tendency of poetry has been notably in the direction of the *poem of political protest.* Formally, it appears as a recitative poem (Erich Fried), as song and *chanson*, as an expansive montage structured to describe in sweeping arcs or to tell a story.[39] The rejection of nearly all the traditional "contents" that still appear in isolated instances in lyric poetry runs parallel to the steady growth of the political poem of protest. This can be expressed more forcefully: today, there seems to be general agreement only with regard to protest. At the same time, distrust is on the increase against all forms of that structure that people have traditionally designated as poem or song. Distrust of the aphoristic short poem with its superabundance of dark metaphors; distrust of an easily mastered montage technique; distrust also of the exactly predictable models of the political poem.[40] Political poems are always pro or con. In the West, con. This is often intended with bitter earnestness.

It is also intellectually fashionable. With its socio-political tone, it creates a socio-political alibi, a nice unburdening of the personal conscience.

"Truth can be expected of man," Ingeborg Bachmann said in 1959 at the awarding of the Prize for Radio Plays given by those blinded in the war. It would be possible to apply this sentence with variations to contemporary poetry. The political poem can be expected of man (both writer and reader), as can the resigned withdrawal from society (writer). But this does not answer the question, "Where to live today? and how?" The poem that is metaphysically and hermetically directed inwards (Celan) will probably endure only as a rarity. The political poem struggles either for a better democracy or for revolution.[41]

# 2

# *Wind Hens Interrogated*

Grass is known chiefly as the author of *Die Blechtrommel* [The Tin Drum], of *Hundejahre* [The Dog Years], of the story *Katz und Maus* [Cat and Mouse], perhaps even of the play *Die Plebejer proben den Aufstand* [The Plebeians Rehearse the Uprising].[1] But he began as a lyric poet. Among the important writers of his generation, he is the only one who has published and had success with all three forms of literature: epic, drama, lyric. In addition, he has written literary essays and delivered political speeches, or speeches in which literature and politics were combined. Does that mean that Grass is, for the time being, the last "all-round" writer in the German language? Until someone else appears, it would seem that he is.

## *The Advantages of Wind Hens*

Grass's first volume of lyrics was published in 1956 under the title *Die Vorzüge der Windhühner* [The Advantages of Wind Hens]. As a kind of textual gimmick, the title poem was more than an original inspiration. It stated a basic attitude toward the lyric; it contained a kind of poetics.

*The Advantages of Wind Hens*

Because they take up scarcely any space
as they roost on currents of air
and don't peck at my tame chairs.
Because they don't disdain the hard rinds of dreams,
don't run after the anagrams
that the postman loses every day before my door.
Because they stand still,
from breast to tail feather
a patient surface, written small upon,
no feather forgotten, no apostrophe . . .
Because they leave the door open,
the key remains the allegory
that crows from time to time.
Because their eggs are so light
and digestible, transparent.
Who ever saw this moment
when the yolk has enough, puts its ears back and
keeps silent.
Because this silence is so soft,
the flesh on the chin of a Venus
I nourish it.–

Often, in an east wind,
when the partitions are swaying,
a new chapter is unfolding,
I lean happily against the fence,
without having to count these hens,–
because they are countless and steadily increase.[2]

Who are the wind hens? What are their advantages? Of the eight sentences in the poem, six begin with and the last ends with a clause introduced by the word "because." This series of clauses is the structural backbone of the poem. The poem affirms, argues. It affirms the "advantages of wind hens":

Because they take up scarcely any space . . .
Because they don't disdain the hard rinds of dreams . . .
Because they stand still . . .
Because they leave the door open . . .
Because their eggs are so light . . .

> Because this silence is so soft . . .
> Because they are countless and steadily increase.

Even the other statements in the principal strophe—with the exception of the second sentence from the end: "Who ever saw this moment . . ."—are linked elliptically with the conjunction "because": because they "don't peck at my tame chairs," because they "don't run after the anagrams that the postman loses every day before my door," and so on. While he is directly affirming the advantages of wind hens, the lyric *I* is indirectly characterizing them and giving them form. And they are, in fact, very much in need of affirmation and form. From two elements of the external real world, the poet has constructed a third—the art word, the metaphor "wind hens." Their reality does not rest upon either the one or the other level of the two basic words. Something new has been created. The wind hens are creations that have been visualized, formed, invented, not made in imitation of nature, but abstracted; they are, in the literal meaning of the word, artistic creations: as insubstantial as the wind and as fruitful as hens; more tangible than the wind, yet closer to spirit than to any hen roost; docile, patient, clever, open, transparent. Fantasies of the poet, products of his imagination, openings, outlets, production and construction of the spirit. The "key" to them "remains the allegory." To what does it point? Only to the building elements, the filterings, the imaginative compounds of the poet—or also to the filtered world? The "postman" and his "anagrams" belong to the externally real, not to the imagined world. "The flesh on the chin of a Venus" seems to be intended as a comparison or metaphor for the "soft silence" that is a product of the wind hens, of the artistic construct. The poet's tactile sense is apparent. In a poem that is so laden with metaphors and that seems to have no other end than the artistic construct itself, even the "east wind" and the "fence" of the last strophe seem to belong not so much to the external, real level as to the artistic and metaphorical level, to the level of the montage framework that has been hewn, filtered, and erected almost entirely in the imagination. The bridge to the world is thin and problematical.

The poems themselves are "wind hens," imaginative constructs. Just as there are sonnets about sonnets, so "Die Vorzüge der Windhühner" is a poem about a poem, about Grass's production in verse. For this reason, the creator-ego is able to look "happily" at his wind hens, call them his own with the air of a connoisseur, display them. Wind hens are superior to plump hens on a roost "because they leave the door open" to the reality that is presented and to be interpreted, to the reality that has provided the building elements, because they are "a patient surface" for the inclusions and exclusions of the poetic imagination. The eggs are words. It is for this reason that they are "so light / and digestible, transparent." Like eggs, words have a double point of reference. On the one hand, hens are products of eggs, just as poems are products of words. On the other hand, hens lay eggs, produce poems; the imaginative idea produces the individual word. When the eggs, when the words, have "enough yolk," when they are ripe, they become silent: the moment of fulfilled silence. The artistic construct rests upon itself. This is not the place to introduce a comparison with Mörike's poem "Auf eine Lampe" [To a Lamp]; with the beginning of Rilke's *Stundenbuch* [Book of Hours]: "The hour is approaching"; with Goethe's "Zueignung" [Dedication], which was conceived as the introduction to a religious epic "Die Geheimnisse" [The Secrets]; with Hölderlin's "Mein Eigentum" [My Portion]; or with Ingeborg Bachman's poem "Mein Vogel" [My Bird]. In all these poems, poet and poem, the relationship of the art construct to reality, the relationship of the poet to the divine, to the world, and to his fellowmen are treated as themes, as is the poetic process, which is called "inspiration" or (more commonly today) a "sudden flash." It seems significant to me that no upward glance to a divinity, no positive communication with this world and its inhabitants are to be found in the poem about the wind hens. Grass's poetic ego leans in isolation against the "fence." "Nourishment" and "multiplication" of the wind hens, the happiness of him who cares for them and has constructed them, take place in a wind chamber that reveals itself as just another floor or just another mode of construction of the former ivory tower.

"Bird," "yolk," "egg," "pullet," "hens," "crow," "yellow," "flesh," "patience," "chairs," "happiness," "wind" recur in the linguistic field of the volume that takes its title from the "wind hens." The pictorial metaphor of the bird assumes a central place. The allegorical prose fable, "Fünf Vögel" [Five Birds],[3] varies and broadens the theme of the wind hens. The "five birds" are shown in their "childhood," in their professional activity, and from the point of view of their twofold goal.

From childhood, so we are told, these birds have been innocent. Hardly were they born when they were appropriated by the grown-ups, ordered to their purposes, used as objects. Is this world capable of accepting young living creatures except as data for use and quick schemes?

> Five birds. Their childhood meant: be a pole, cast shadows, be nice to every dog, be counted, everything stopped at five, seven had to be situated in America and America?—Here began the great journey, the lasting transformation, which in the end means the egg.

In the second part, the five want to "look for work." It irks them to live without *élan*, to subsist as impudently and unimaginatively as sparrows off the "currency," the "gold on the street," the "horse" apples. Such things belong to the level of the worthless, the ordinary, the dependent. The birds are searching for a more active, more lively, more sophisticated relationship to the world. They are helped in their endeavor by their unlimited protean nature. They can offer themselves "as chimneys" to "smoke" for a factory; they can "assist the telegraph office in making long distance calls"; or temporarily replace the "five missing fingers" of Löffler, who delivers papers; or set up the "five-poled tent for a circus"; or let themselves be used as "pillars" for a bank; or "take over a wharf" in Hamburg and work as "cranes." Wherever they work or settle, the five cause confusion. With purposeful glee, they confound relationships, break their contract, and travel restlessly on. Migratory birds and "casual workers." Modern goblins, more powerful than those in fairy tales, intentionally mischievous. Author and birds achieve their goal: parodistic satire. Satirical parody. Pleasurable revenge. With innocent expressions, they sprinkle sand into the machinery of the grown-ups; determined to work with them, yet not to work with them, to disturb. They "interrupt . . . long distance calls," let "the façade of a bank collapse," inaugurate a "strike" on the wharf. On each occasion, their disruptive action is successful and mischief results. With such superiority, it is a pleasure to be alive. The world is powerful, but the birds are more powerful.

The world is stupid and the birds are wise. The world is wicked. But the birds have their fun with the wicked. "In these days (that is, of the strike), the visa arrived. The great journey could begin." The next station *ex machina.* This time, the scene takes place in America. Part three:

> The five had gone out to look for the seven. In Virginia, on an apple farm, they found the seven. They joined them. They moved in near to the seven and built a happy fence. But then along came D. S. Abraham Brothers, to whom the farm belonged, who loved freedom and hated fences. He had his saw and hammer with him. He sawed off the seven and rammed the five into the soil of Virginia. He made everything nice and smooth again with bulldozer and roller.

The goal toward which the birds travel is more or less identical with their own happiness in a happy Arcadia of the twentieth century. The age-old dream mixed with provocation and demonstrated with rhetoric. The birds are shown to be, by birth and behavior, the truly free, the republicans, "freedom" as a trademark, a philistine lie. The free farmer of the U.S.A. "hated fences." This world has no understanding for the freedom of bird-Bohemians. It allows no Arcadian tents to be pitched in its midst; it wants to have its farm "nice and smooth." It is in favor of order and against the revolution of idle loafers. And yet, the use of "saw and hammer" cannot harm the five birds who can fly out of harm's way. For the present, these, who are perhaps the last martyrs and heroes, are immortal.

> But the birds float in the air in some astonishment between coal and saltpeter. They find no more work. Therefore, they next decide to lay and hatch five eggs, one for each continent. Who knows what might be found between albumen and yolk. In any case, the eggs ought to be full of impressively strong surprises for Europe, America, and the other continents.

Without work and kept from Arcadia in a world that values activity, the birds begin their second mission. In the beginning, they were a kind of demolition crew. Now they proceed more surreptitiously with what is, so to say, their own production. Now they "lay and hatch" what used to be called the salt of the earth, later genius, or, according to circumstances, fertilizer or even explosives. Under the author's whispering, they bring their "eggs" into the world, want to provide for "impressively strong surprises." Will the birds free the world from its stupidity with their ideas, will they punish it for its lies? As the truly productive, will they found a kingdom of truth, of justice, and of peace? A messianic kingdom of "birds"?

The mobile and witty birds are a cipher for the artist, his malaise, his feeling of injury and his cultivation of this feeling, for the dissatisfaction, the protest, the demand for freedom, the kaleidoscopic wit, for the commitment of a contemporary artist type. The "five birds" are the defendants of Arcadia and the mandrake egg; they represent a plea for the birth of a better world, for childhood and intellect, innocence and criticism, for the wish-reality of studio and imagination. These birds alienate themselves from the common "sparrows." The egregious "swallows" are "unbearable" to them, the dung of "sea gulls" is repugnant to them. Their own existence is more open, more peaceful, more shrewd, more aggressive: a synthetic metaphor, half esoteric, a cipher. Rascals.

Something similar was already to be found, although in a quite different vein, in German romanticism. Not as though the world ridiculed by the birds were a justifiable world. But, apparently, the birds and their demands are not justifiable either. The question is whether and to what extent the world is that which the montage fable shows it to be. An author as gifted as Grass can achieve much with rhetoric. He can give words a pejorative meaning by juxtaposition and arrangement ("currency," "gold on the street," "horse" apples); by his choice of metaphor, he can construct a montage framework for the world, play jokes with the parts of the montage, attack vaudeville figures with a stick-from-a-sack, and present himself as a frustrated "jolly good fellow" and a promising world betterer. To repeat: the question is what such a construct, such a procedure, and such a play instinct on the part of the director of the birds have to do with reality. The claim of injustice actually endured, of anger really justified, and of a real need for betterment on the part of the world is expressly stated in the text. But who is the object of the birds' sense of work and play? Are they not maliciously self-satisfied in the role of bogeyman? Do they really believe that they can hatch a new world egg? I find the birds' claim and a world construct like the one shown here very unconvincing. In such a poem, words and sentences play primarily with themselves. A kind of intellectual self-satisfaction. Too much pubescence: neither childhood nor adulthood. There was a time when that would have been called artistic narcissism.

Grass's lyric and his use of the egg as theme are apparently influenced by Hans Arp.[4] Arp's play instinct influences by its modesty and innocence, by the play form proper to it. In Arp, it is possible to detect the successor of a Novalis or a Brentano. Grass, in his play, gives notice of a direct attack on society. He turns the full force of his water hose into the faces of the bourgeoisie, washes them, and forces their necks into his collar. Content and form of these verses point to satire. But satire, if it is to be effective, must concern itself with reality. The higher the moral claim and the sharper the protest, so much less can satire be satisfied with an artistic revel. In Grass's early works, a fatal mingling of play and reality, of caricature and life, is often to be found.

## *Gleisdreieck*

Grass's second volume of poems is called *Gleisdreieck* (1960).[5] It is printed in a large format and decorated with drawings. In conjunction with the hen metaphor in the first volume, Grass had already mentioned "Dreiecke" [triangles] and had juxtaposed "Gleisdreieck" [a triangle formed by tracks] with "Adventslied" [an Advent hymn].[6] In the second volume, his tone has become harder. His exuberant play instinct functions with more difficulty. The line, "My hens do not laugh," is repeated like a refrain in the poem "Geflügel auf dem Zentralfriedhof" [Fowls in the Central Cemetery] (G 61). The second volume also takes its name from the title of one poem. In a "Gleisdreieck," tracks come together from different directions, meet, and separate again. It is a place of much traffic. In Grass's poem of this name, a huge spider sits in and above the *Gleisdreieck*, the metaphor and allegory of evil power. It lives, works, supervises, and controls. It "lays the tracks" (at the crossing point from one sector to another) and repairs them. Only the cleaning women are permitted to go "from East to West." The spider's enlarged "gland writes: / Gleisdreieck, You are now leaving / Gleisdreieck and the West Sector." It is possible to hear the loudspeaker.

"Gleisdreieck" is both a place in Berlin and a metaphor for the division of the city. The fact that "cleaning women" who work for the German Railways of East Berlin (the elevated railway in the whole of Berlin belongs to the East German government) ride into West Berlin is insignificant for the life of the city, a grotesquerie. The giant spider spreads its net under the warning shield. It catches "what falls into the net" (men) like "flies." *Gleisdreieck* ought to serve to link men together. Here it separates and threatens them. The meaninglessness of this arrangement, the evil of the guardian spider, becomes visible. That was so even before the wall was erected. "The tail light (of the trains) means me." The speaking *I* and his friends are all affected. They belong to the "we" of the divided city. Bitter reality has been given form in this poem. It is a relevant poem on a contemporary issue. Grass never relinquishes the theme of Berlin—and this shows how intensively he lives in Berlin and feels himself identified with it. The volume *Gleisdreieck* begins with a poem about Berlin. "Brandmauern" [Fireproof Walls]:

> I greet Berlin as I
> beat my forehead three times
> against one of its walls (7).[7]

These are the walls that were bombed in the last war. Toward the end of the volume, the author lets the "great woman of the rubble" speak:

> Grace grace.
> The great woman of the rubble
> has conceived a plan
> to which every stone will submit.
> The great brickmaker is willing to cooperate (97).[8]

What is the great plan? "To free the city," to rebuild Berlin. The woman of the rubble recruits helpers. But her "beaux" refuse, they want no part in this common endeavor. The "great woman of the rubble" dies. The author "pronounces her a saint." In the third volume, *Ausgefragt* [Interrogated], it is not the "Brandmauern," but the huge new wall, the "Wall," that is the theme of the lament, the protest, the powerless rage.[9]

The second volume also speaks often of the egg and of hatching.

But there is no mention here of the eggs of the "wind hens" or of the "Five" who are so adept at transformation and so shrewd in their revenge and their travels. It is the world as egg, or, more exactly, life as egg, a primeval concept of humanity, an archetype. The wind hens do not hatch, nor do the five practical jokers. This is not the open space of artistic phantasy with which one can cope, but the space with which one cannot cope, the closed space, man "in the egg" and the writer whose "pencil" has, it is true, cooperated in the hatching, but which must also let itself be hatched.

*In the Egg*
We live in the egg.
On the inside of the shell
we've scratched indecent drawings
and the first names of our enemies.
We are being hatched.

The one who is hatching us
is hatching our pencil too.
Some day, when we're out of the shell,
we'll immediately make
for ourselves an image of our hatcher.

We assume that we are being hatched.
We imagine a good-natured fowl
and write school essays
about the color and breed
of the hen that's hatching us.

When will we get out of the shell?
Our prophets in the egg
dispute for a moderate sum
about the length of the hatching period.
They postulate an X-Day.

What is the nature of the activity of those in the egg? The themes of sex and faeces in Grass's works, as well as the aggressive instinct of his heroes, are well known from his novels. Here, too, the first strophe vindicates the analysts of sex and of the drive to power. But in any event: "We live in the egg," and "we are being hatched." A little intellectual relativization—for we are honest—seems to have been applied to today's egg-dweller: "We assume that we are being hatched." Between the two statements is the threat: But we'll write up the process, pursue it critically, "make for ourselves an image of our hatcher," institute a complaint if necessary. Nevertheless, "we imagine a good-natured fowl." Distance is lent to the hatcher by the use of the general, unspecific noun "fowl." Is this to be regarded as the elevation of a comprehensible idea "of the hen that hatches us," or as a lowering and a mild affront?

The usual type of school essay about the "hen" confirms, at any rate, the pedagogical triteness of an opinion that is both formed and formative. It is understandable that Grass attacks it. Does his brood hen contain a transcendental, religious reference? The Biblical overtones of the expression "make . . . an image" point in this direction. Yet the poem makes an effort to be cautious. It seems, at the same time, to be criticizing the general "assumption" that "a good-natured fowl . . . is hatching us." But what is the object of the alienation—the good-natured fowl, or the generally-held notion of the good-natured fowl, or both? Probably both. Blows in both directions, and the critical and skeptical intellect ruling like a king despite all restrictions. On the other hand, a word from the Bible, a word of Christ's, seems to be linked to the passage by association. "Jerusalem, Jerusalem, thou who killest the prophets and stonest those who are sent to thee! How often would I have gathered thy children together as a hen gathers her young under her wings, but thou wouldst not! Behold, your house is left to you desolate" (Mt 23, 37–38). At one and the same time, the words are a lament and a judgment, a statement about a particular situation and a prophetic speech, a reminder of earlier threats (1 Kgs. 9, 7 f.; Jer. 22, 5). But in Grass's work, there is nothing of the terrible and unequivocal claim that is found in the Biblical utterance. Even when he is criticizing only the idea of the other (which in this case is not difficult), the believing Christian ought not to evade the issue, or at least ought not to be satisfied with the mere assumption of a "good-natured fowl." Throughout the poem, he must remain aware of the challenge in Jesus' words. "Prophets" like those in the poem can be treated ironically, can be laughed at, can be declared not too intelligent. They "dispute for a moderate sum / about the length of the hatching period. / They postulate an X-

Day." First, the discrediting of the prophets ("for a moderate sum," and "dispute"), then the relativizing indefiniteness of the statement. What is the "X-Day" of escape from the shell? What does it signify? What is the dispute of the "prophets"? What do they say? Is there really a day of escape? Or is it only a vague hope? A grotesque irony on the part of the "good-natured fowl"? What could a day of escape mean in this poem and in the context of all the poems? The day of human maturity (what would that mean?), of death? of the transition into true openness, into transcendence? the day of Christ's return for the world-egg? The "day of Yahweh" in the Old Testament is plainly understood as the day of God's judgment. But that can hardly be what Grass means. In his poem, the escape from the shell can mean only an escape into that space of preconceived freedom and happiness that is never precisely named and never positively depicted, that is more an Arcadia of the poetic fantasy than a political reality or even a salvific reality. The lyric *I* gives no further details about the actuality, possibility, or probability of X-Day. We cannot visualize either it or its meaning with any clarity.

In the next two strophes of the poem, there is a new perspective, a new beginning. We have escaped from the shell, we "invent" and "are very much worried about our progeny in the egg."

From boredom and real need
we have invented incubators.
We are very much worried about our progeny in the egg.
We would gladly recommend our patent
to the one who watches over us.

But we have a roof over our heads.
Senile chicks,
Embryos skilled in languages,
talk all day long
and still discuss their dreams.

Incubators speed up the hatching process and are supposed to make it safe. Apparently, "the one who watches over us," the hen, is not interested in "our patent." The next strophe points out by way of apostrophe that there are "senile chicks" and "embryos" that talk the world and themselves to pieces. That is one of the platitudes.

The question would be whether "we"—and that includes the lyric *I*—belong to them or not. Does this *I* consider itself once more superior to such a world and does it, therefore, except itself? It seems so. If "we" were the implied subject, the last line, to be grammatical, would have to read "and still discuss *our* dreams." As it is written, however, it reads: "*their* dreams." So it is the others who are senile, chicks, stupid.

In strophes seven and eight, there is a return to the original perspective. Back into the egg.

> And what if we're not really being hatched?
> If this shell never breaks?
> If our horizon is and will remain
> just the horizon of our own scratchings?
> We hope we're being hatched.
>
> Even though being hatched is all we talk about,
> it is to be feared that someone
> outside the shell may feel hungry,
> break us into a pan and sprinkle us with salt.–
> What will we do then, you brothers in the egg? (G 30–31).[10]

The last strophe (the eighth) introduces a new relationship. Here there is no longer a reference to the relationship "egg-brooding hen," but to the relationship of the egg to "someone outside the shell," who, perhaps, "may feel hungry, / break us into a pan and sprinkle us with salt." That means someone on whose activity we are dependent. The allegorical image is extended. A powerful someone, a power other than the big hen that influences the egg, a power that can intervene in human fashion, that can exercise authority over the hatching process and hinder it.[11] By association, this is closely related to the concept of one who consumes us politically. "What will we do then, you brothers in the egg?" Here, too, the question remains unanswered. Experience, reflection, criticism, hope, fear, question—all developed with reference to the egg metaphor. The metaphor combines the concept of the world as egg with that of life as egg and with the developmental process of a society.

Grass makes an important statement about his own attitude to the poetic in "Racine lässt sein Wappen ändern" [Racine Has His Coat of Arms Changed] (G 58–59). It is a reflective narrative poem.

The world of birds and hens is met here in the form of the "swan." In the poem, Racine includes a "swan" and a "rat" on his coat of arms. "Above, the swan, / below, the rat." "Friends ask (Racine) about his swan, / but mean the rat." The swan stands for grace, for what is innocently pure, for the sublime, for "beauty" in the classical sense. It is true, "Swans sleep / where it is shallow, / and Racine understands that part of his coat of arms / that is white / and serves as a pillow for beauty." He understands the rat less well, and the day comes when he no longer has any understanding of this rat, which "is a water rat." It "starts gnawing / with its teeth from below / on the sleeping swan." "The swan rises up screeching, / rends the water, / moonlight is impoverished and Racine decides / to change his coat of arms." He removes the rat from his coat of arms. "But its absence leaves a void thereafter in the coat of arms. / White, silent, and ratless / the swan will sleep through its cue." Without the dark, the uncanny, the impure, without the unsleeping rat, without its teeth, its bite, without its disturbance of sleep and of the peaceful moonlight, "the swan will sleep through its cue"; classical beauty will lose its suspense, the author of dramatic "verses" will lose his productivity. The "ratless" beauty of the swan becomes "white" and "silent." If Racine removes the rat, then he must, to be logical, "renounce the theater." No productive ability without the rat, without its nightly prowling, without its wounding bite? Grass has described the foundation of classical beauty, has named the problem of bourgeois beauty.

### *Interrogated*

Even the *Windhühner* volume had contained a "Credo," had treated with irony words once held sacred, and had contrasted them with secular details. The verses of "Credo" pay homage to the "wind-quiet room," to the "pious cigarette," to the "mystically" effective consolation of both. The speaking *I* believes in the concrete and cozy everyday world, sketches a peaceful vertical onto the horizontal, an idyll without God. It is not the Holy Ghost Who ascends and descends, but the cigarette smoke, the spider on its thread:

pious, a cigarette,
it believes vertically,

vertically the spider a plummet
explores every shallow . . . (W 47).[12]

In the *Gleisdreieck* volume, the poem "In eigener Sache" [In My Own Cause] is presented in answer to a reproach. The reproach:

People say:
He wants to take the future away from the cocks,
He's as concerned about hens
as if it were a question of improving the egg.

People say:
He believes in fowls.
The Holy Ghost greets him
in the form of a hen.

The answer to this reproach:

That's all wicked slander,
the truth reads like this:
Sometimes I have a toothache,
then I feel better again;

especially on Sundays
I am certain
that such an allusion
can also give pleasure.

But later, when this tooth
no longer presses on the one nerve,
I chew worry
and look at the blackbirds
—it doesn't have to be
cocks and hens—
until I see black before my eyes (G 77).[13]

If I understand this rightly, Grass is saying, in answer to the reproach in the second strophe, that he does not employ the figure of the hen to conceal or alienate the dove as a symbol of the Holy Ghost, and that the hen assumes for him neither the place nor the significance that Christians accord to the Holy Ghost and His symbol. To the reproach in the first strophe, viz., that he is constructing an anthropology, a cybernetics, and an aesthetics of hens, Grass answers—and this is typical of him—only indirectly. He refers to an objective experience, to a toothache, concedes with a smirk that, "especially on Sundays," the "allusion" to the relationship of the "hen" to the "Holy Ghost" ". . . can also give pleasure"; that, for the rest, his "worry" outlasts and outweighs his toothache; that he does not cling unreservedly to the visual present and future of hens; that "blackbirds" also suffice to make him see "black before [his] eyes." One must recall here that Grass was, at this time, already working on *Hundejahre*, and that one of the principal narrators and heroes of this work is called "Amsel" [blackbird]. Eduard Amsel, in *Hundejahre*, is the builder of a world of scarecrows. As a New Year's greeting to his customers, Amsel, as the manufacturer Brauxel, sends them the maxim written on deckle-edged cards: "The scarecrow is made in the image of man." That is to say, man provides the norm for scarecrows. The grotesque is made according to the image of man (not of God). The hen lies hidden in the egg, man in the scarecrow, the aesthete in the contemplater of hens, one's "own cause," that is, the cause of the artistic present and of the human future, lies hidden in the anxiety about the egg and the hen.

It is striking to note how difficult it is for Grass, in all his works, to free himself of Christian names and symbols. Upon occasion, his deflowering of Christian names and references, his witty contrasts, turn out rather badly. In the poem, "Zauberei mit den Bräuten Christi" [Magic with the Brides of Christ], "the Holy Ghost appears" to a nun "not in the form of a dove" but in the form of a "sea gull" that "pecks out her eyes." And the comment is made about all the nuns walking on the seashore: "What they call heavenly bridegroom is known elsewhere as bogeyman" (G 51). Unquestionably, this poetaster who plays with verses, images, and references does not know Who that "Spirit" is Who was promised and sent by Jesus Christ, what the "pneuma" of the New Testament promises and demands, what the "pneuma" of Paul discerns.

The volume *Ausgefragt*[14] contains the poem "Der Delphin" [The Dolphin], "dedicated to the Apostle Paul and to Peter Weiss." The theme of the poem is conversion. The Jewish Saul was converted into the Christian Paul. Peter Weiss was converted from bourgeoisie to Marxism. A third person, Alfred Döblin, whom Günter Grass designates as his teacher, was converted from a bourgeois, Socialist writer into a Christian, and finally into a Catholic. "Like Saul," but unlike Paul, Alfred Döblin, or Peter Weiss, Günter Grass discovered in himself "the docile dolphin" that could leap, dive, and swim itself free:

> Obediently, I saw my teacher poised to leap:
> the convert behind the microphone.
> Heard him abjure and laughed his confession to pieces.
> Pupil's laughter. Dolphin's laughter.
> Ridiculously he turned himself upside down.
> Then I was, today I am.
> Yet when he had vomited stale cake
> and served up fresh rolls,
> like Saul just after the molting,
> I discovered the docile dolphin
> in me—I leaped!—
> when I was supposed to believe in it, supposed to believe in it,
> fear soured my laughter:
> I made sure of the exit,
> dived, and swam myself free.[15]

The speaking *I* of these verses "laughed to pieces" the "confession" of his teacher Döblin. This confession is to be found in Döblin's "Epilogue" (1948): "I, the erstwhile worshiper of the world. . . . The truth, only the truth can make us whole. . . . But we allow ourselves no rest. We cannot resign ourselves. Our crazy spirit cannot be still. That is its inheritance from Cain. Each one of our days repeats the fall into sin. And yet our spirit dreams and hopes that it will reach something, it knows not what. Satan goes among us. We cannot doubt it. . . . But the eternal, good, and just God does exist. Only in His presence is the horror comprehensible. It is obvious how much we have detached ourselves. The oppression, despair, and misery of earth call to Him. . . . The eternal God—called 'Jesus' among us—immersed Himself once in our flesh and ignited the true fire of old in this barren vessel."[16]

The speaking *I* of the poem "Dolphin" designates and describes his laughter as "Pupil's laughter. Dolphin's laughter." In the rest of the poem, the pupil's laughter is not mentioned again. Grass, in his lecture on Döblin: "An author has to cultivate hiding places." The idea of the dolphin's laughter is developed. The convert Döblin—each convert including, therefore, Peter Weiss?—"ridiculously turned himself upside down." Grass's ego, on the contrary—the lyric *I* is here an existential *I*—"discovered . . . just after the molting," that is, after the conversion and development, "the docile dolphin" who could "swim," "dive," and "swim itself free"; and, therefore, "when I was supposed to believe in it, supposed to believe in it, . . . I made sure of the exit." Even more strongly than the undeveloped concept of the "pupil's laughter," the line "fear soured my laughter" relativizes the "exit" that the *I* gains by diving and swimming. The sentence from the prose story "Five Birds" is also relevant here: "Believe this, believe that, here there is doubt" (W 39). But the absolute that is contained in this sentence seems to have been relativized in the later poem by the "pupil's laughter"—for the pupil is still and only a pupil and the teacher a teacher—and by the "soured fear." It is permissible to ask whether the freedom of the dolphin is the author's last freedom, his last "Credo." I venture to doubt the finality of the dolphin, especially since this dolphin already has his "guardian angel" (cf. the poem "Mein Schutzengel" [My Guardian Angel], A 46). The dolphin, his leaps, and his freedom signify nature and art. Is this *I* already leaping, kicking against the goad?

The title poem of the third volume is called "Ausgefragt" [Interrogated]. It is the first poem in the volume. "Interrogated / after great and small anger," the *I* answers the questioner's questions:

> How do things look?—They've looked worse.
> Were you lucky?—Thanks to the bait.
> And what have you done since?
> Books tell how things can be done better.
> I mean, what have you accomplished?
> I was against it. Always and ever against it.
> And became guilty?—No. I didn't actually do anything.
> And did you perceive what could be perceived?
> Yes. I perceived rubber with my fist.
> And your hope?—I lied the desert green.
> And your wrath?—It tinkles like ice in a glass.

Shame? We greet one another from a distance.
Your great plan?—Didn't pay off so well.
Did you forget?—Recently, my head.
And nature?—I often drive past it.
Men?—I like to see them in films.
They're dying again.—Yes. I read about it . . . (A 6–7).[17]

Who is this interrogator? In what direction do the answers point? Is the interrogator, perhaps, not so much a second social person as that side of the *I* itself that demands an accounting? Is the poem, then, rather a self-interrogation and self-address? Perhaps a contemporary variant of a Baroque sonnet "An sich selbst" [To Oneself], such, for instance, as a Gryphius might have written? In the Baroque period, even the sonnet that was formally a monologue could not dispense with society. Conversely, the poem "Ausgefragt," which is formally a dialogue, cannot dispense with the address "An sich selbst." The interrogator comes from outside, begins with the customary generalities, then moves into more personal areas, into the question of action, guilt, recognition. Nonconformism and "wrath" are affirmed. The interrogator serves the balls to the answerer, Ego II to Ego I. Both are trying to formulate the framework of a confession. Although the poem is more realistic than Grass's earlier attempts (e.g., in "Five Birds"), more comprehensive than the references to details in "Credo" or "In eigener Sache," less prone to escape into witticisms, it is not without its *pointes*. Despite its satirical tone, and not without understatement, partial satisfaction, and deliberation, "Ausgefragt" formulates the position of a man in middle age. Satire: "Men?—I like to see them in films." Lament and sober statement: "And nature?—I often drive past it." Even the *memento mori* is sounded for the first time. "They (men) are dying again.—Yes. I read about it. . . ." Despite the querulousness, disappointment, and playfulness, there is much affirmation of life in Grass's works. "My big yes forms sentences with a small no" is the title of a whole cycle (the only cycle to date) in the volume *Ausgefragt*.

Despite all the banal details and ironic linguistic aberrations, "marriage" also belongs to the big yes that "forms sentences with a small no."

Between Anna and Anna
I choose Anna (A 14).

Who is Anna? Edgar Allan Poe wrote an immortal love poem, "Annabel Lee." And that is also the title of Grass's "Hommage à E. A. Poe" (G 93). There is also the grotesque montage love poem by Kurt Schwitters, "An Anna Blume" [To Anna Blume]. Perhaps Grass was thinking of the two Annas in Bertolt Brecht's "Die sieben Todsünden der Kleinbürger" [The Seven Deadly Sins of Towndwellers]. "One of the two Annas is the manageress, the other is the artist; one is the saleswoman, the other the wares"; one is intelligent and businesslike, the other "beautiful," a "dancer" who gives herself to many men. Between the former (Anna I) and the latter (Anna II), Grass decides for a third Anna, for his wife, to whom he had already dedicated *Die Blechtrommel.*

## *Object and Doubt, Play and Commitment*

Grass combines objectivity in detail with play, play with doubt, doubt with commitment. Play as artistic expression and procedure. Doubt toward the reality of the historical and the present. Objectivity as the experience of concrete, mostly ordinary, things, as the reality comprehensible to the human senses.

To a striking degree, the comprehension of little things means a taking hold of them, the comprehension of opportunities means remembrance. Obviously, not in the sense of a Hölderlin or a Rilke. There is no lyric wholeness in the traditional meaning of the word. One searches in vain in these verses for superimposed values and referential systems. Wholeness and lyric shrewdness are concealed in the details, or are submerged by much understatement and the erection of unexpected relationships. The great lyric themes: nature, presentiment of immortality, the inner space of the world, the German forest, the capitalistic jungle of the metropolis, the motif of the outcast, the claims of a book of devotions, the adjuration of the new man, an ideologically conceived political utopia—all these are missing in Grass's poems. As an ironical contrast to political poems of protest, as a contrast to the new ostentation of lyric poets who dabble in politics, as a counterfoil to the "do something" (A

59–63), that is, to the anger in their poems, Grass speaks his "yes" (to mention but one example) to "pickled pig's head" and complements the lyric recipe for anger in the poems of protest with his own lyric recipe for "pickled pig's head" (A 64–68). In *Windhühner*, Grass had already expressed his interest in cooking and in the joys of the palate in the poems "Bohnen and Birnen" [Beans and Pears] and "An alle Gärtner" [To All Gardners] (cf. Enzensberger's "An alle Fernsprechteilnehmer" [To All Telephone Subscribers]). In *Ausgefragt*, he opposes "a level soup spoonful of middling wrath / in boiling salt water" to all the lyricists' political recipes for "just anger" and "powerless wrath" and to their "anthology" of "napalm" metaphors (A 60); the smaller "flame" under the cooking pot to the great flames of napalm; to all the lyric afterwords and P.S. speeches, he opposes his "economic postscript" on how to utilize leftover scraps of food to prepare "a tasty soup . . . that can provide a simple but nourishing meal for families with many children" (A 68). Is Grass opposing an unfashionable ease to the fashionable malaise? Is his naked finger pointing out the bourgeoisie to the professional non-bourgeoisie? Has Grass no further protest to utter? Or is it rather his sense of reality that compels him to distrust the "industrial market," the new lyric buskin, the napalm museum, and the mortuary precisely as industrial market, buskin, and mortuary?

In the poem "Diana—oder die Gegenstände" [Diana—or the Objects], Grass has expressed rather directly the meaning of the *objective* in his poems (and in all his works). Diana the huntress, as Artemis, sister of Apollo, shoots her arrow of inspiration into (surprisingly) the "soul" of the poet. Objective correlation:

> When she hit me,
> her object hit my soul,
> which is like an object to her (G 73).[18]

Tension arises between the "resting objects / that my knee bumps on Mondays" and Diana, who "lets herself be photographed only running and among dogs." She strikes "the objects of nature" (nature, in this instance, does not have the meaning that it has in German Romanticism or in the German nature poem), but she also strikes "stuffed objects"—that is, art objects, as, for instance, wind hens. And now the poet's confession in favor of the objective and what can be concretely experienced:

I have always refused
to let my shadow-casting body
be wounded by a
shadowless idea (G 74).[19]

The "shadowless idea" falls victim to Grass's doubt.

Grass accuses the opportunistic political poem of protest of a lack of concreteness. That does not mean that the "political landscape" is excluded from his own poems. But it must be our own landscape, the landscape of the Federal Republic of Germany, not the rhythmic protest against or for a distant land. It is not inconceivable that, in the writing of such a poem, the author's irritation may spill over into the lines, his anger may bubble out of the pipes of the studio-castle. And his political preferences become obvious.

*Political Landscape*
For us wounded, for whom knowledge
is hard to unlearn,
geography arranges confused history:
Beside Adenau and as far as the river Hunte,
Between Galen and Frings,
the Sozis book small gains
make great efforts to unlearn.

The closing of these political lines:

Wherever serious mountains stand in the way
and thought is not fledged,
it's worthwhile to glance
from Blessing across the Rhine.
O, you tributaries, left and right:
the Barzel flows into the Wehner,
Sewage feeds the Sein.
Grauwacke, Rehwinkel, fretsawed Tannen,
Karst, Abs, and Kulmbach beer,
Old Franconian clouds over Heidegger-land (A 72–73).[20]

Such verses belong to the same category as the "Materniads" of the *Hundejahre*—but stop short of the "cruncher's" anger. They are not great verses, but sentences more or less on the level of the mediocre political poems written, for instance, in the period of *Vormärz* (before the revolution of 1848), and destined, perhaps, to be just as quickly relegated to forgetfulness in the cellars of literature. Wholesale judgments by the "wounded" man of the street—or the literary campaigner. Sentences beautified, it is true, by the cosmetics of rhetoric, but not, therefore, more differentiated or more meaningful.

In Grass's works, *play and commitment* have their own peculiar linguistic attitude and tone. The individuality of his verses is evident. Their artistic quality does not reach the level of his great prose. Except for some of the early poems, the tone of the verses is, in fact, particularly unimpressive. A craftsman's joy in language is joined to insight, tells stories in verse, moves in the direction of political *engagement.* The combination of such an extreme play instinct with such a definite political *engagement* is almost unique in the history of German literature. This lyric studio is a castle with play corners, pleasure courts, hen houses, protest towers, built-in kitchen, and a pool for dolphins. The speaking *I* loves the concrete, the objective, the detail, the free combining of fanciful elements, the caricatural distortion. It hates the great metaphysical lyric metaphor, likes to show the goad, to lift the garment and shield of reservation, to shoot the unexpected arrow, to hoist the worm. By instinct, it ogles the freedom of the bird and the potentiality of the dolphin, knows the vital cunning of the egg, forms contrasts based on the principle: "To see all heads in cross-section./ When a shark swims in profile across the picture./ Or hairs stand on end in a cross-current" (A 39). In his poems (and in his prose), Grass writes against the idea and what proceeds logically from it, viz., ideology. Skepticism, the individual experience dependent upon the senses, and a vital play instinct threaten ideological wholeness, mitigate ideological rigidity. Against humorless adults, he introduces the "doll" into the field (cf. G 41–44); against image and garden fence, he injects his satirical "scarecrow" into the game (cf. G 34–35). Grass uses his verses to frighten man away. The "poet" warns against himself. "Wicked / as only Sütterlin script can be wicked,/ he expresses himself on lined paper" (G 38). Or more aggressively: "My tongue lashing / is Baltic spiteful room-warm" (A 90).

Against a shadowless "yonder," he projects his "shadow-casting body" (G 74). With verses like "Who wanted redemption, / called for the doctor or for milk? / Now they are coming: priests and ambulances, / nurses and nuns./ With proverbs and carbolic acid. . . ." (G 69)—with such verses, it is not hard for one who is sure of his own vital strength to find concurrence for his views. But how will he view the task of being man when, one day, his own athletic lyric ego must include itself among the "half-used athletes" (G 68)? Undoubtedly, he will be compelled, then, to reach another foundation of reality, another level in his experience of reality. It is primarily "the good God" Whom his verses want to frighten away. "Under the coffee cozy sits the good God / and cannot stop / becoming gradually cold and angry" (W 46). As in the case of Brecht's youthful works, this is not the God of the Bible, but of the bourgeoisie, the God under the coffee cozy, Whom the bourgeois has first warmed, tidied up, restricted, and rendered harmless. But the attack against the "good God" is, according to Brecht and Benn, a cheap—according to Barth and Bonhoeffer an untheological—notion, a mock cavalry attack on grandfather's tin soldiers. Here, too, the concurrence of the reader seems to have been purchased at too easy a price.

In 1960, on the occasion of a public discussion in Berlin on the topic: "Lyric Poetry Today," Grass called himself a writer of "occasional poems." "What annoys him most are poets who cannot wait for the occasion, the gentlemen in dream laboratories, the gentlemen with copious excerpts from dictionaries, the gentlemen—it could be ladies, too—who work from dawn to dusk with language, with linguistic material, who live garrulously like permanent boarders in the vicinity of silence, who are always on the track of the unutterable, who call their poems texts, who do not want to be called poets but I know not what, who—let us say it—are without occasion, without a muse."[21] As a lyric poet, Grass pays no heed to the inner space of the world, to "smoldering days"; he is impervious to contemporary grammar, to contemporary experiments in combining series of words, and to the possibilities of alienation thereby afforded. He has devoted himself to occasions, stories, sudden ideas, observations of the world around him, the philosophical poem (and, therefore, reflection), the aphoristic *pointe*, even to allegory, and finally, to the political poem. Grass seems to use the expression "Gelegenheitsdichter" [writer of occasional poems] as a counterconcept, opposed to the concept of the professional lyricist as the term might be applied to Rilke, Benn, Krolow, Celan, but also to Heissenbüttel or Ernst Jandl.

Günter Grass's three volumes of poetry are separated from one another by more than a decade. Is it possible to speak of a *development* in lyric attitude, in linguistic tone, in objectivity? Even in the second volume, the attempt to settle on an artistic free stage, on (so to speak) the level of the "wind hens," was already less noticeable. In *Gleisdreieck*, reality had become more concrete. It was not interpreted so unequivocably as correctness of detail. It was obviously Grass's experience of a bombed and politically divided Berlin, where men were confined and their existence questioned, that brought about the change in his poetry. The volume *Ausgefragt* shows that the *I* of the poems has become increasingly involved in a social and political reality that is not to be overshadowed by the play instinct of artist or of cabaret. The sentences in these poems are unusually understandable and direct. The taming of a play instinct that is so marked, so rampant, so firmly entrenched in its studio-castle and so eager to deform the world is a wearisome and by no means small moral undertaking. Volume by volume, the wrath becomes more modest; even the tragic makes its appearance ("Mein Freund Walter Henn ist tot"; "König Lear" [My Friend Walter Henn Is Dead; King Lear], A 29–31). The sense of democratic political reality rejects both those who write poems of protest and those whose protest, even in verses, is revolutionary (A 75 ff). The lyric *I* confirms: "My big yes forms sentences with a small no." Calm flows into the verses. On all sides, "Wrath boils away with the soup" (A 69, "Epilog"). "Don't decorate - write," demands the writer. The speaker demands: don't formulate protests, be politically active.

The superiority of the studio is no longer played off against powerlessness and anger. Artistic freedom no longer compensates for the lack of what is livable and real. The "magic" with verses, with "wind hens," "scarecrows," and "brides of Christ" has ended. It is hard to predict what kind of poems Grass will write in the future. No new possibilities of form seem to suggest themselves to him.

New themes? Perhaps the problem of concurrence with a ruling party? It will be interesting to see whether the late Brecht or the late Döblin will someday provide the new inspiration, whether and how Grass will remain Günter Grass.

# 3

# *Lyric Poetry Today?*

*A report on the Current Discussion about the Lyric*

Is there still any justification for lyric poetry? Why should anyone write or read lyric poetry today? Some are asking: Why not participate directly in the action, the knowledge, the construction of things? Those who say this belong to the doers, to the direct consumers. The others, the aesthetically initiated, reject this "why?" Lyric poetry is art. All art is an end in itself; not useful, but very necessary, "blessed in itself." The poetess Hilde Domin inserts her experiences with the lyric, her reflections, and her spirit into the lacuna between these two extreme positions.[1] Her remarks provide the most significant statement about lyric poetry to appear in Germany since Gottfried Benn's lecture on the "Problems of Lyric Poetry" in Marburg in 1951 and reflect, far more than Benn's remarks did, the contemporary social scene, "literature and readers in an administered society." Undoubtedly, it is only those who, on the one hand, are aware of the academic discussion about lyric poetry or who, on the other hand, are aware of Höllerer's "progressive" attempt at lyric poetry who can venture to inquire into or to assess Hilde Domin's treatment of the lyric.

In Germany, since the war, the academic discussion of the lyric has rested on two basic works, on Emil Staiger's *Grundbegriffe der Poetik* [Basic Concepts of Poetry] and on Hugo Friedrich's *Struktur der modernen Lyrik* [Structure of Modern Lyric].[2] Staiger, working primarily from the German romantic tradition of the *Lied* [song], defined the lyrical element as loneliness and that which appeals to the lonely, as mood, disposition, soul, sound, as singing and interiority, as the absence of distance between subject and object, as union. "Thinking and singing are not compatible." "One who is lyrically inclined assumes no attitude." "There are no contours in the lyric. Everything flows into everything else." The inference is not far to seek: a poem is a poem only insofar as it is lyrical. Staiger has rejected this inference. But can one dispute the dramatic as an essential element of drama? Staiger has not produced enough evidence to show what lyric poetry might be outside of and without the lyrical. Speaking, discussion, irony, proof have no place in poetry.

Hugo Friedrich, professor of Romance literature at the University of Freiburg, approaches the structural description and analysis of the modern lyric from a study of Baudelaire and the French Symbolists. Since he rejects the critical concepts of classical poetry (harmony, inner serenity, lawful proportion, raising of the individual to the status of the universally human, ability to ennoble, dignifying of the emotions, and so forth), Friedrich is obliged, for the sake of consistency, to work with negative descriptive concepts. These concepts were used as non-censorious categories even in the romantic period, especially by Novalis. Friedrich enumerates the following categories drawn "from German, French, Spanish, English writings on the contemporary lyric": disorientation, dissolution of the familiar, loss of order, incoherence, fragmentation, reversibility, parataxis, depoetized poetry, destructive flashes, striking images, brutal suddenness, dislocation, astigmatic (distorting) vision, alienation." He mentions the grotesque in poetry, the ugly, the empty ideality, abstraction, codes and arabesques, the subject's claim to power, the dictatorial fantasy, lyric as contradiction, silence and irony, lyric as anchoretic "*poésie pure*," as a mingling of the real with the dream and with the absurd. In German poetry, however, these concepts are applicable only until Surrealism, only until Rilke, Trakl, and

Benn. About Brecht, Heissenbüttel, and Enzensberger, that is, about the poets who have become known since 1950, they tell us nothing. Nor do they tell us anything about Arno Holz and most of the Expressionists. "Political lyric" is expressly excluded since Friedrich's discussion extends only to 1950. In the poems and authors whom he analyzes, the urge to freedom is one-sidedly determined from the point of view of "fantasy." Such a poem has largely withdrawn from society; it is both unable and unwilling to address itself further to society.

In *Wege der Forschung* [Paths of Research], Reinhold Grimm has summarized the present academic discussion about the lyric in German-speaking countries.[3] This volume too, which includes Staiger and Friedrich, ends chronologically with the disciples and variants of French Symbolism, with Trakl, with the German nature lyrics of this century, with the discussion about Mannerism, with metrical and rythmical considerations, with Benn. With a single exception, the really contemporary poem has found no entrance into this study. The Frenchman, Pierre Garnier, himself a lyric poet and critic, gives a report on the concretist program of Gomringer and the Brazilians. Concretism is not, however, really discussed, analyzed, or shown in relation to other forms of the lyric. The contribution is isolated in the volume and removed from the academic discussion.

The peak of the academic discussion and reflection about the modern lyric was undoubtedly achieved during the workshop "Kolloquium Köln" [Cologne Colloquium], inaugurated in 1964 by the research group "Poetik und Hermeneutik." Professors from all existing areas of specialization took part in it. The lectures and discussions were published under the title *Immanente Ästhetik. Ästhetische Reflexion.*[4] Chronologically, the area under discussion was the whole of "modern" lyric from 1850 to 1920. The study reaches farthest into the contemporary period in Heselhaus's "Brechts Verfremdung der Lyrik" [Brecht's Alienation of the Lyric] and the discussion that it engendered. This is the first great study of Brecht's lyric to emerge from the West and, from the formal point of view, it is the most rewarding to date. In it, Heselhaus provides a masterful demonstration and analysis of Brecht's forms of alienation in relation to Marxist "estrangement" and to the "alienation" of Russian formalism in the 20s and of Chinese dramatic art. As both method and title indicate, the social relevance of the lyric poems discussed in *Immanente Ästhetik* is either extraneous to or on the periphery of hermeneutic reflection. A hermeneutics more strongly oriented toward sociology would take exception to this state of affairs. In the philosophical introduction ("Thoughts Based on Hegel"), Dieter Henrich expresses regret that there exists almost no productive relationship between the philosophical interpretation of modern art and its interpretation by the artists themselves. But this observation, according to Henrich, might also serve as a reminder that we are "to regard the most recent developments (of art) as beyond the doubtful patterns of advancing decay and anticipation of progress."

In the winter of 1966–1967, Walter Höllerer invited "authors of progressive literature" to a Literary Colloquium in Berlin. He has since edited and published the results.[5] Paul Celan, Hilde Domin, Günter Eich, Franz Mon, Peter Huchel, Ingeborg Bachmann, Hans Magnus Enzensberger were not present. In an Afterword, Höllerer describes the broad spectrum of the authors included: "Authors with scientific, reflective methods. Ecstatics, social analysts, adherents of mysticism, technicians of sentences, those whose absolute is onomatopoeia, critics of history, authors of far-reaching visions, of exact particular observation, authors who argue politics." It is, in fact, astounding to what extent writers of poetry differ among themselves. The Swede Lars Gustafsson (b. 1936, translated into German by Enzensberger), whose works appear at the beginning of the volume, writes: "It is time to rub metaphysical sleep out of our eyes. . . . The tragedy of man, as of machines, lies in the fact that he has no mystery." The Frenchman Yves Bonnefoy (b. 1923) confesses: "For me, this is poetry: to make visible in the bread and wine that nourish us the presence of the holy." Heissenbüttel, on the other hand, says: "What I would like to show are possibilities that reveal a formal side, but that lead, at the same time, into the meanings of words." The Yugoslavian Miodrag Pavlovič (b. 1928/, a writer from the Socialist bloc, still believes in the "enigmatic anthropological roots" of literature.

Heinz Piontek, in his review of Höllerer's book (in the newspaper *Süddeutsche Zeitung*, December 7, 1967), distinguished three directions among the poets represented: first "those who demolished sentence structure, the experimenters and players, the monomaniacs of language, whose principal and major theme is language itself." To this group, Piontek assigns the Austrians Artmann, Jandl, Mayröcker, as well as Heissenbüttel and the Italian Sanguinetti. To the second group belong those "who still rely on the power for statement and proof that is inherent in the sentence, who want to make themselves comprehensible, who still have something they want to *say* to us." In this group, he includes the Poles Różewicz and Herbert, the Yugoslavs Pavlovič and Popa, the East Berliner Kunert, the Russian Vossnessenskij, the Frenchman Bonnefoy. The aged Francis Ponge and the LSD initiated Ferlinghetti in the United States might also be added to this group. A third group "obviously sees no reason for assuming an extreme position. It makes its decisions about form as the occasion arises and tries to bring the playful into harmony with the committed, the artistic with the strongly grotesque, even with what belongs properly to the cabaret." This group includes Piontek, Grass, and Rühmkorf, the Czechs Holub and Hanzlík, the Americans Olson and Creeley. It is apparent that these three directions cut straight across political camps.

"Despite all the differences of literary tradition, social background, and individual attraction," Höllerer sees "one distinguishing mark at the center: the writer admits that the language of everyday has a lawful place beside the artistic languages of calculation—and that both produce real effects and meanings." That seems to me to be an important insight. Today's lyric poets are faced more imperatively than earlier ones with the problem of language, with its unproved assumptions, with what is spent, brittle, porous, and possible in language. They force sentences in traditional or everyday language through the literary engineer's linguistic and stylistic mill, through the filter of linguistics, and into the new (often plastic instead of ivory) towers of the artistic. Höllerer assigns his authors to the "realistic" school of literature. He defines "realistic literature" as that which "forms some awareness of what actually happens and what can happen." Höllerer's definition of realism provides an ample framework. Within the framework, however, questions must be asked. What does "actually" happen today? What "can happen?" Who sees it? Who determines it? The respective secretaries and archbishops of literature, who are unanimously opposed to "dogmas" but far from mistrusting their own dogmatism? According to Höllerer, his various authors purpose "to approach the present without reservations carried over from yesterday." With magnificent aplomb, he fails to consider what yesterday was or was not; whether the so-called present does not, in its own way, sometimes mean exclusion and reduction; whether it does not sometimes bring tendentious perspectives, a narrowing of the intellectual and linguistic vision; whether and to what extent, to phrase it differently, the present as such is already a qualitative concept; to what extent it is, or can be, the object of reflection; to what extent its concept of the present, formed by hotel and group tours, participates after its own fashion, in the attitudinal, the fashionable, the intellectually half-proved, and must defend itself for this participation before history and before the coming generations.

In this area that is overlooked by Höllerer and no longer considered in the academic discussion, Hilde Domin asks, from an intellectual standpoint that is rare today, about the reality, the potentiality, the necessity, and the need for the poem. Sociologists and psychologists adapt man to a predetermined mold. The poet does what he has always done: he experiences reality, diagnoses the potentialities and conditions of life, points out changes in consciousness, probes walls, investigates wishes. Archaic poets were able to name the nameless. They sat in the sun of poetry, in Arcadias. Today's poets, in a world full of named things, must name the unnamable, query obscure names, unmask false names. They appear as critics. On the edge of silence, the real poets, those who are not just rhetoricians, reveal themselves as the real speakers. "Insofar as the lyric binds us to ourselves, to our real *I*, it also binds us to others, gives us once more the possibility of communication." For Domin, the prerequisite for such poetry is the meeting of the author with his own existence, the achieving, at least for moments—which then reveal themselves as decisive—of identity with oneself. The intellectual place of the poet today is "between." Between the attitudinal patterns of a society that is administered "diachronically" and "synchronically," that is, between the traditional forms of life and the society that is oriented toward the past and administered from within on the one hand and, on the other, the society that is administered from without "by a system of front-rank, same-rank, and rear-rank men," by "utility clubs" and "groups." He stands on the "crosswires," "in the dilemma of two rival dialectical processes, on the edge of two social structures, keeping watch for a third. He stands, therefore, by his own choice, at the crossroads between the old order and a possible utopian order. For that reason, the lyric poet of today must be one who resists, who says 'no,' who cannot 'extol'; his 'yes' is present as the potential of his belief in the permanence of his existence as man. . . . Without this 'yes,' without the secret utopia of his own potentiality, which includes the potentiality of others, no word of poetry could be written today. Or read." Therefore, the lyric, which was understood "earlier as 'flight from reality' or as a 'conservative utopia,' becomes, in an age of adaptation and synchronized administration from without, a prerequisite for the construction of human society per se. . . . Against the 'one-dimensionality' of an adapted and resistanceless functioning."

Domin, too, sees the lyric as "an object for use," although she does so less superficially and less tendentiously than Enzensberger and with the difference that, to her, the poem, not as a commodity but as a "magic object for use," shares in the inexhaustibility of spirit and form.

In all of today's literature, there is an "uncanny machinery for shaping judgments." The great publishing companies, the feuilletons, the literary groups are not so innocent in this regard as they often claim to be. What we call good taste has been in a critical conditon for a long time now. Because of this crisis in judgment and taste, people "are calling" today more loudly than ever "for norms." The cry is "a despairing rejection of one's own power of judgment." And norms, for the most part, are uncomfortably close to being ideological measuring rods. Even the "mottoes drawn up" by literary groups, "which in the beginning were real team maxims wrung from the practice of the best writers," manifest "more and more frequently the character of ideologies."

As criteria for the lyric of yesterday and today (and for literature in general), Domin names "*authenticity*," "*individuality*," "*exemplariness.*" "*Authenticity*" is understood as the "absence of untruthfulness"; that is, the poem "must be true with reference to the concrete reality of the experience through which it has passed and which has filtered, constructed, or even transformed it." Truth in word is "the agreement—in the very moment of formulation and without the application of any violence, however it may be motivated—of the experiential content that is to be formulated with the formulation that is to be chosen for it. In other words, a point by point correspondence on a sliding scale." "Sliding" because it occurs "after the loss of idealistic absolutes." "*Individuality*" is something unique, unexchangeable, at once the archetype and the model, the exemplary per se: the exemplariness of an "unrepeatable and unique experience of reality" and "uniqueness in formulating it." "*Exemplariness*" excludes "words chosen arbitrarily or for external reasons," is linked to "necessity," and is "inseparable from authenticity and uniqueness."[6] In an aside, a criterion is offered for the poems that are current today and that consist of mere description or (skilled) rhetoric. Verses and texts without "uniqueness" provide "nothing but patterns," perhaps "two-dimensional precise outlines—models of perception. Or perhaps working models, purely technical, applied presentations." But they remain outside the "potential area of art." "Uniqueness is the blood that these outlines drink, their three-dimensionality (that is, authenticity, individuality, exemplariness) is their life." The criterion of individuality is related in Domin's thought to tension and life, to intensity, to the entrance of an ego into existence. One of her predominant attitudes toward "current literary questions," which she presents as "notes in a feuilleton," observes "that it is precisely 'individuality'—and with it the possibility of art in general—that is in a state of crisis today and that the writer is in danger of excluding his own individuality, which contains his very existence, in favor of (mere) professional understanding or ironical exaggeration."

Lyric poetry today? Although it cannot do without the "apparatus of information," it is nevertheless still in the "quiet zone of truth." Lyric poetry as a means of "resistance to neutralization" and as the "courage to proclaim one's own identity." Lyric poetry "more skeptical than Brecht," who wanted to change reality and society with his lyrics; "more confident than Benn," who regarded art as being without consequence. Lyric poetry as the "breathing space of freedom" in the administered society. With great exactness, Hilde Domin has described her own position between an ecstatic, interior lyric on the one hand and a purely constructable, rhetorical, and politically external lyric on the other. Between the doers on the one side and the contemplators on the other, she is a lyricist who reflects and can offer reflection; who, although professionally informed (with regard to both society and literature), can still say "heart"; who admits creative knowledge into her thought processes; who does not woo for public favor or for the favor of or membership in established literary groups. Both lyrically and analytically, Hilde Domin has a voice of her own: freedom in a limited space.

# 4

# *Group 47*

## *Report and Critique*

People have asked and are still asking: who or what is Group 47? Some critics have called the Group's members the "young wellspring" of postwar German literature; others have reviled them as "a horde of Communist moles," or have sought to unmask them as "paper tigers" or as a "Reichsschrifttumskammer" (Nazi agency for writers). Among gentlemen, they have been labeled not "fit for the salon," "shirt-sleeved," "literary rowdies." By still others, they have been regarded as a youth movement of people no longer quite young, as a postwar Storm and Stress movement, as anti-Western, as disturbers of the peace, as the beginning of an extraparliamentary opposition. People have both praised and feared their machine for awarding prizes or executions, their "electric chair" before the whole assemblage. Later, people accused the Group of being a "commercially organized, demagogic managing body," and of possessing the "vanity" of a coffeehouse clique. The Group appeared as a "closed society" with singularly open doors, as a club with no roster of members, as a group of "ideologists with no ideological program." The epithets, categories, and labels—they did not fit this literary establishment. For here, in the magic horn of the German alphabet, something new and intellectual was at work.

Is it strange that the Group appeared to some as a literary "Mafia," to others as a kind of Ku Klux Klan? Independent observers, the professional press, were not admitted, except to the recent meetings in the host countries of Sweden and the United States. Anyone in Germany who has reported about the meetings has also been a participant in the meetings: members, friends, guests who were in one way or another linked to the Group, representatives of particular interests, or those who have since been expelled from the Group. Some members of the Group, the vociferous—the majority of them are newcomers—have spread an aura of pretentious superiority about themselves and have acted as if they alone were the leaven, the only true leaven, of the society. Although the Group, for reasons that were initially valid, had at first refused to allow observers, "the noise of the press," at their meetings, they have, since the end of the 50s, been courting publicity in a variety of ways. Those who had joined the Group because they wanted to reflect, discuss, prove; because they were passionately committed, were soon enough pleased—and some members contributed thereto by no means unintentionally—to have their brand new names linked to the Group's literary prominence and, consequently, to the ruling midday.

"Gruppe 47," Christian Mayer-Amery wrote in 1966 in the New York journal, *The Nation* (Vol. 202, No. 20, p. 588), ". . . comprises about 80 per cent of the mainstream writers of today's Germany. . . ." Who or what is Group 47? There are innumerable answers. We might take a "middle" one by Wolfgang Hildesheimer, who as a "member" ought to know all the answers. "Group 47, as everyone knows, but only those of good will will admit, is a circle of writers who share with one another not necessarily their personal or literary sympathies, but certainly their political idiosyncracies, who meet once a year in order to read their works aloud to one another, to criticize one another, and to assure one another, by the very fact of their being together, of their solidarity."

"Confused by the favor and hatred of the parties, his character wavers in history," Schiller said of his hero Wallenstein. A party picture, a prosaic two-party picture, has, to a large extent, established the image of Group 47: here, the friend in a white shirt (red tie, or none at all), knowledgeable, open, young, progressive, worthy of trust; there, the enemy, in a black [academic] gown, disgruntled, untractable, dogmatic, dealing in abstractions, or so it appears from the perspective of friends. From the perspective of the enemy, there are "prefabricated successes," "journalistic tricks" (G. Blöcker), "lack of norms," "a phalanx of consolidated promoters of their own interests" (R. Neumann), "German provincial inbreeding with a comic claim to world significance" (H. E. Nossack).[1] In the beginning this was not so. Group 47 had a beginning. It occurred in the postwar years.

### *DER RUF and the Founding of "Group 47"*

In the years just after 1945, one might have heard, among the older writers and among those formed in a Western and Christian spirit, a call to reflection and change; one might have discerned a finger pointing to "eternal laws," to tradition, to the West in its humanistic or Christian meaning. Newspapers like *Die Wandlung* [The Change] or *Neues Abendland* [New West] bore titles that were symptomatic of the tendencies of the age. *Die Wandlung* appeared in Heidelberg in 1945. It was edited by Dolf Sternberger and contained contributions by Karl Jaspers, Ernst Robert Curtius, Alfred Weber, Marie Luise Kaschnitz. *Neues Abendland* was started in Augsburg in March 1946 and was edited by the Catholic Wilhelm Naumann. For a public that wanted nothing so much as rest, survival, stabilization, progress, stability after the millionfold killings and separations, after the total shock and confusion—for such a public, the stabilizing and ennobling tones of these Western-oriented journals raised a far-reaching echo. In the years of Lucky Strikes, chewing gum, black market, it was comforting to recall the West as the bearer of culture, as the bringer of light to the world. By the end of the 40s, there was already a tendency to feel reassured about the rediscovery—whether real or surmised—of tradition. Needs, tendencies, and reassurances found their political expression in the founding of the Federal Republic of Germany in 1949. Historians are aware of the difficulties and achievements of those years. But "what became apparent in the second and third year after the war," wrote Golo Mann in his *Deutsche Geschichte* [German History], "was the strength of the bourgeoisie or of the 'restorative forces,' as they were called. The exaltation in which people believed that they could and must begin everything anew did not endure for long."[2]

Not everyone, in those years, found it possible to decide in favor of a traditional Christian or bourgeois humanity, to find assurance in the mirrors, decrees, watchtowers of a newly-found tradition. As returning soldiers, these men were distinguished from the older populace by their age; they were distinguished from other returning soldiers of the same age by their more strongly altered awareness. They were no longer able to believe that patterns of thought and behavior could so easily be appropriated from the past. They were no longer willing to work obediently to acquire the heritage of their forefathers. They were convinced that their fermented spirit had to find new ways and forms. Since they found few plans prepared and ready for their use, they experienced difficulty in giving concrete expression to their ideas and goals. But they were determined to go their own creative way.

Later, the collective tradename given these restless ones was "Group 47." The nucleus of Group 47 was the journal *Der Ruf* [The Summons], edited in Munich by Alfred Andersch and Hans W. Richter. Its subtitle read "Independent Pages by the Younger Generation." The first issue appeared on August 15, 1946. The "germ of *Der Ruf*," Hans Werner Richter reported in retrospect, "originated with Alfred Andersch, Walter Kolbenhoff, Walter Mannzen, and others in the POW camps for Germans in the United States. Nearly all of these men were from the Socialist camp, had been strict opponents of National Socialism, though they had had to serve it as soldiers, and believed, in the first postwar years, in the possibility of a new beginning for Germany. Their criticism of the thesis of collective guilt, of the re-education and de-Nazifying policy of the American military government on the one hand, and of the Socialist machinations of dogmatic Marxism on the other, put them between both camps. They were opposed to Stalin's barren theory of equal power and public ownership, to which every human freedom would have to be sacrificed, but they were also opposed to every kind of bourgeois restoration, which threatened to suffocate every new impulse. Their belief was in a new kind of democratic Socialism." About the end of *Der Ruf*, Richter writes: "In April 1947, it was forbidden by the American military government, on the basis, or so one assumes, of Russian intervention, and it was then newly edited by Erich Kuby."

The journal that Andersch and Richter edited under the name of *Der Ruf* had several times drawn upon itself the unfavorable notice of the American "Publications Section." The freedom of the press to which the editors laid claim was directed, in some instances, against the occupation forces. These, in turn, accused *Der Ruf* of hidden "chauvinistic" tendencies. The "suppression" of *Der Ruf* has since become legendary. As yet, no attempt has been made to give a more exact presentation of the tensions between the editors of *Der Ruf* on the one side and the military government on the other. *Der Ruf* was published by the Nymphenburg Publishing House. The founder and license holder of the firm was Curt Vinz. Mr. Vinz informed me briefly: "Actually, there had been from the beginning—that means, then, from the era of Andersch and Richter through that of Erich Kuby and even into that of Walter von Cube—objections and even more or less veiled threats of suppression, or, more correctly, threats that my license would be revoked. But there was no suppression of the paper or strict order to dismiss its editors. For the departure of Andersch and Richter, the determining factor was, in the end, differences of opinion between the publishing house, the editorial staff, and the journal's free co-workers. In the opinion of the publishing house, the journal reflected too much the (subjective) opinion of the editors."[3] So much for the correction of a legend that is still in the process of formation.

Hans W. Richter emphasizes in retrospect: "The origin of Group 47 was political and journalistic in nature. It was not literary men of letters who created it, but politically committed journalists with literary ambitions. Their purpose can be understood only in terms of the collapse of the Third Reich and the atmosphere of the first postwar years. They wanted, under all circumstances and for the whole future, to prevent a repetition of what had happened, and they wanted, at the same time, to lay the foundation stone for a new democratic Germany, for a better future, and for a new literature that would be aware of its responsibility for political and total social development" (A 8). It is permissible to ask if anyone could have been found, in those years, who did not want to prevent "under all circumstances and for the whole future . . . a repetition of what had happened." People wanted that in Heidelberg, too, and in Augsburg. The new fathers of the Federal Republic also wanted it. In those years, such a wish was far from being a *specificum* even among writers. It belonged to the stylizations affected by certain leaders of the Group to say that, whereas earlier poets and writers had all been unpolitical, only those writers who were directly engaged in politics—and, if possible, only those whose Vietnam slogans made a good impression on television—were privileged to write since the founding of Group 47.

The voice that made itself heard in *Der Ruf* was the voice of a generation oppressed by the military government of "democratic" countries and forced by that oppression to remain in the background at the political foundation of the Federal Republic, to remain in the background not only because of the "narrow-mindedness" of the later Bonn fathers, but also because of the military government.

Alfred Andersch, then thirty-two years old, had written in the first issue of *Der Ruf*: "The law under which European youth is placing itself is the demand for European unity. The instrument that it is determined to use to this end is a new Humanism, divorced from all tradition; a belief that makes demands on man and that believes in man, a Socialist Humanism. Socialist—in this case, that means that the youth of Europe stands 'left' whenever there is question of social demands. . . . But the youth of Europe is humanistic in its inexhaustible hunger for freedom. . . . The negation in which young Germans are living is not a sign of a definitive triumph of nihilism, but its opposite. . . . Its solution can already be voiced: their educators must be brought up to date." This youth demands "right thinking" and "the kind of life it engenders," an "unbroken existence" after the pattern of Sartre. It is opposed to the poverty of thought manifested by those who cultivate tradition and by the American concept of "reeducation." It demands the "other way," the "way that is our own" (R 22 ff.). Hans W. Richter formulated it thus in the second issue of *Der Ruf*: "A generation is silent! It is silent because people do not want to understand it; it is silent because it cannot understand. Between the not-wanting-to-understand and the not-being-able-to-understand lies a world, lies experience, lies war, lies the timeworn question about human existence that was ruptured, that was quickened by the experience, and that seems, in the second half of this century, to be making current once more all the intellectual bonds of the West.... Man, who yesterday was the lord of creation, has today become questionable to man.... His image is disintegrating before the terrible experiences of this age.... Even the finest speeches of the professors fail to convince us that this disintegration of a well-ordered human image is not taking place.... This generation knows that the image of man that the older generation inherited from its forefathers and would now like to construct again cannot be reconstructed. It knows that this image has been totally destroyed.... And so man, ruptured in his relations to the world around him, doubting and erring in his existence before God, before the universe, before himself, steps once more into the center of life, must again be made the resting pole of a new social existence....' It is the image of that man that must be born out of the feeling for life of the younger generation" (R 30 ff.). In the same issue, Walter Mannzen wrote about "the self-alienation" of man, about the incentive that comes from Marx, about "healing." "Healing, if it is possible at all, is possible only from the roots up. The root that must be considered is to be found in the economic sphere. Healing requires that the economy be freed from the shackles of profit and business mechanisms and that it be controlled by planning. Yet all this is only a prerequisite for healing.... Once the daily bread has been assured, everything depends on free development and on man's right to self-determination in the use of all his faculties. Only the broadening of man so that he becomes a person, not a function, is important.... The only way to remove self-alienation is through self-realization" (R 41 f.).

Self-assured, idealistic, critical, courageous sentences are to be found in the first issues of *Der Ruf;* many sentences reflect the clear vision of their authors; others are condemned to utopia, and not always through the fault of others. Students also came under discussion: the student "is predestined to be a revolutionary *par excellence.* A revolutionary, not a fighter against barriers, but a critic, an experimenter and—when the time comes—a reformer. For most students, as we have seen, the 'time' has not come" (R 93).

That sounds young and beautiful, "Europe" and the "new man," "free development" and "healing from the roots up." At the decisive moment, the group associated with *Der Ruf* did not succeed in concretizing itself politically—not because others were against it, but because the forces and the determination needed for such a concretizing were manifestly lacking. One must agree with Golo Mann that "German—West German—bourgeoisie came to power for the first time with Adenauer" (992). "To earn" for the country and "its maligned dignity a measure of autonomy, a respected place in the world, interior order, prosperity, peace and again peace—that is the extent of his conscious goals; they scarcely extend further" (Golo Mann, 994). But why were the leading writers of *Der Ruf* so easily satisfied with rancor, polemics, sulky interjections? Why were these dynamic men so immovable? Why did these men who were so inventive, so gifted in cunning, seek for no dialogue?

In September 1947, Hans Werner Richter invited the former co-workers of *Der Ruf* to a meeting on the Bannwaldsee near Füssen. Those who were invited read to one another from the manuscripts that they had brought with them. They discussed the founding of a new literary journal. It was to be called *Scorpion* and was to appear on January 1, 1948. A sample copy had already been printed. But the United States government refused to grant a license on the grounds that the journal was "nihilistic." Both the Rowohlt and the Blanvaley publishing companies had been competing for the publishing rights. Heinz Friedrich, who was present on the Bannwaldsee, reports that "no one had at first thought of forming a group" (A 19). In fact, however, this meeting saw the birth of Group 47. The name presented itself only some weeks later. Hans Georg Brenner invented it. At the next meeting, on November 8–9, 1947, friends and others of similar interests met as "Group 47." "Hans Werner Richter, who was fascinated by the idea of a community of writers without the status of a society and without a general secretary, was its founder. . . . The politicians of *Der Ruf* had become literary pioneers. The year 1947 brought the change. Or was it the beginning of an inner emigration on the part of these courageous journalists, of an emigration into the fields of literature after their political action had failed?" (A 21). So queries Heinz Friedrich, who was present. No one will deny that these men had courage. But did an "inner emigration" at this moment of time demand courage? As a turning point, it was momentous; as a fixed point, it was the beginning of disappointment and crystallization.

### *"Ideal Starting-Points"*

Very few members of the Group would deny that there were "ideal starting-points" that they held in common. The renunciation of a formulated literary, or literary and political, program does not exclude a basis of common convictions. Nor does it have to be, in every instance, a matter of "renunciation" and "asceticism." Hans Werner Richter himself accepted and formulated these mutually held "ideal starting-points." In his retrospection in *Fünfzehn Jahre* [Fifteen Years] (1962), he emphasized the fact that Group 47 "was stamped from the beginning with the same mentality" that had given rise to the postwar journal *Der Ruf.* Richter has described as follows the faith, hope, and aspirations of the associates of *Der Ruf:* "Their faith was a new kind of democratic Socialism. Their hope was the restoration of German unity and the uniting of Europe, the hope of a new democratic, socialist Europe led by those 'teams' [Equipen] that had arisen in all the countries of Europe after the war" (A 11).

Richter knew that Group 47 "had experienced some mutations in the course of its existence. But its ideal starting-points remained firm.

They were :

a) to train an elite group by democratic methods in the fields of literature and journalism;
b) to demonstrate repeatedly the practical application of democratic methods in a circle of individualists, and to do so in the hope of achieving a long-range effect and perhaps, much later, a far-reaching effect on many people;
c) to achieve both goals without a program, without a club, without an organization, and without giving support to any type of collective thinking" (A 11).

The words "without a program" must also be seen in their historical perspective. Hans Mayer remarks with justice that "the renunciation of a literary or even a culturo-political program had its origin in the 'total suspicion of ideologies' that marked the years in which the Group was founded. People were determined to regard reality without the assistance of any prevenient philosophical concepts: neither pre-established harmony nor disharmony. . . . But this program of ideological asceticism was in itself an ideological program" (A 31). Richter does not tell us "whether and to what extent Group 47 achieved, even partially, the lofty aims that it had set for itself in the first postwar years, or even if they were actually attainable. They were never expressed, even within the Group. They were immanent from the beginning. They had been passed on as self-evident by their predecessors, the editing staff of *Der Ruf*" (A 11).

Although Enzensberger and other authors later claimed that Group 47 was lacking in "aesthetic doctrine," in "the normative feature, the fanatic unanimity" (A 25), the older Richter admits candidly: "If the individual was not equal to the literary or critical—or often even political—standards of the Group, or if he could not do justice to its 'traditions' or mentality, then the invitation (to attend a meeting of the Group) was not repeated" (A 12).

There can be no doubt about the fundamentally democratic and socialistic, "anti-Fascist and anti-authoritarian . . . tendency of the Group" (A 13). From this basic orientation came its antagonism to the "restorative powers"of the Federal Republic of Germany, to those forces of authority that had either remained in power or been reinstated, and to the "dogmatists." The campaign against literary trash, against "Blubo" literature (the "blood and soil" literature of the Nazi period) was an indirect and spontaneous result of the discussions of the critics during the meetings. The campaign against new forms of a political and social establishment was added in the 50s. A tendency that was present from the beginning—to oppose the bourgeoisie (whether upper or lower)—persisted throughout the years. Some of the authors of Group 47 have more than once degraded their political opponent, caricatured the thought that differed socially or "ideologically" from their own, made their opponents seem stupid. They have not refrained from climbing into social or other trenches. They have preferred to shoot at their opponents rather than to seek a dialogue with them. They have consciously provoked . . . and have screamed "ow" when some politicians, not knowing the rules of literature, have struck back polemically. They are not without guilt for the fact that the political parties have been unable to bridge the gap between themselves and the intellectuals. Nor are they without guilt, even today, for the dangerous rift between workers and intellectuals. They have been guilty, and not without a measure of self-satisfaction, of inbreeding. They should have seen and understood that the man on the street cannot live from the table of Group 47 alone, that the worker cannot wait for the bread of Group 47. This understanding, too, would have been socialism.

### *Development of and Generations within "Group* 47"

The first, and perhaps the most decisive, "mutation" for the writers around Hans Werner Richter was that from *Der Ruf* to Group 47. It was the transition from political journalism to literature. The returned soldiers were thwarted, let themselves be thwarted. And this fact produced the first, and never to be surmounted, disappointment of the "team" [Equipe]. The "team" (to use Richter's term) was changed into the "clique" (the term is Enzensberger's).

Today, people are asking why these political journalists did not struggle more vehemently when the opportunity was offered. Later, in the 50s and 60s, they composed explanations, protests, proclamations. But it was not until 1965 that Günter Grass and some of his companions entered the political arena in any concrete sense. Why did those men who prided themselves on their democratic morale fail to struggle harder in the decisive years of 1947–1949? Why did they avoid political concretizing? Was it only the others who were guilty that those men had no share in the formation of the political will and power? Hans W. Richter uses the expressions "shared guilt" and "own failure" in answer to this question. I find the question neither expressly stated nor reflected upon in either the Almanac or the Handbook of the Group. Is it such an unimportant question? The excuse from the pen of Hans Werner Richter comes, despite the question indicated in the half sentence, too easily and too feelingly. "This Young Germany too," he writes, "born of a political impulse with revolutionary goals and broad aspects, was banished or forced into the field of literature, or went willingly into this field because of its own powerlessness and premature resignation" (A 11).

As everyone knows, the road that leads from "political impulse" to political action, from "revolutionary goals and broad aspects" with promises of "See, we make all things new" to the conquest of an extensive intellectual living space is a long one. And it is a road on which one must expect to meet opposition, obstacles, and reverses. Should not the "truth" of the group around *Der Ruf* have been "concrete,"to borrow Brecht's term? Why did not these men, who were politically committed,[4] seek to establish contacts with the political parties that were then in the process of being formed, with the forces that were then being given concrete shape? Idealism can be very beautiful and often very white. But being white is seldom enough.

In the history of Group 47, three generations can be distinguished up to the present. First, the generation of the "returned soldiers." They became the founders of the Group. Second, the generation of those who (as air force auxiliaries or soldiers) were just old enough to have experienced the end of the war. They joined the Group in the course of the 1950s. A third generation, the youngest, did not experience the war or the postwar years. These authors joined the Group in the 1960s, most of them after 1963–1964, when the Princeton caesura had drawn attention to the Group.

To the founding generation belong, besides Hans Werner Richter and Alfred Andersch, Walter Kolbenhoff, Wolfdietrich Schnurre, Walter M. Guggenheimer, Günter Eich, Wolfgang Bächler. Even before the influx of the second generation, Walter Jens and Wolfgang Weyrauch, Heinrich Böll, and Walter Höllerer had joined the Group. The leading members of the second generation are Martin Walser, Günter Grass, Hans Magnus Enzensberger, Peter Rühmkorf, all of them born between 1927 and 1929. They brought to the Group a very strong influx of literary productivity and contributed greatly to the international reputation of the Group. Although they were not born in these years, the following authors belong, if we may judge from their attitude, somewhere between the commitment of the returned soldiers and the new commitment of an Enzensberger or a Grass: Paul Celan, Ilse Aichinger, Ingeborg Bachmann. Celan and Aichinger read their works to the Group for the first time at the famous spring meeting in Niendorf on the Baltic Sea (1952), Bachmann at the meeting in Mainz in May 1953. Even linguistically, the tone of her works places her between the homecoming generation and the Enzensberger–Grass generation. To the third and youngest generation belong such authors as Günter Herburger, Gisela Elsner, Peter Bichsel, Hubert Fichte, Peter Handke, Helga Novak. Also of this generation, although he was born in 1932, is Jürgen Becker, whose prose work "Ränder" [Edges] received the prize of the Group at the "Powder Mill" in 1967. Uwe Johnson, born in 1934, stands between the second and third generation in much the same way as Ingeborg Bachmann stands between the first and second. He was invited in November 1960 to what was probably the first great meeting of the Group in Aschaffenburg; he came, read, was praised, received no prize, left—and has since been living and working quietly in the United States. As yet, the third generation has shown no evidence of possessing a talent as great as that of the second generation, of Grass, Walser, or Enzensberger. At the moment, it is not certain whether Bichsel, Fichte, and Handke are to be counted among those whose literary talent is of the first order.

### *Princeton: Caesura or Swan Song?*

The circle of members, which, in the first four or five years, had increased so notably, soon began to fluctuate. "At half time, more or less between the founding of the Group and the meeting at Princeton—that would be about 1956—only three of the original members were still present, of whom one was Hans Werner Richter, and at Princeton only five of those who had been present in 1956 were still present, including Hans Werner Richter, and of the founding members only one was present—Hans Werner Richter. . . . Group 47, then—they're always someone different" (Hildesheimer, P 111).

One hundred forty authors, critics, journalists, and publishers were invited to Princeton. The seven authors who had been invited from the GDR were not allowed to come. Others were unwilling or unable to come: Aichinger, Andersch, Augstein, Bachmann, Böll, Eich, Elsner, Fichte, Heissenbüttel, Hildesheimer, Walser, Otto F. Walter (H 241 and P 21). Once more, the critics were fully represented: Walter Höllerer, Walter Jens, Joachim Kaiser, Hans Mayer, Marcel Reich-Ranicki. Jens and Mayer had not come to the "Powder Mill" in the Upper Palatinate in 1967. Böll and Walser did not come again after the Princeton meeting. Now Enzensberger, Johnson, and Peter Weiss no longer make an appearance. Richter and Grass were—if one excepts Eich, who obviously wanted to present his new prose works—practically alone with the young writers. The glamour was missing.

Princeton was a *caesura.* It is comparable, or so it seems to me, to the *caesura* that occurred at the beginning when the friends of *Der Ruf* decided to form a Group and a society. Princeton was another, and obviously the last, great concentration of the Group with the stars of the middle generation. The socialistically committed writers were able to travel to New York with $80,000 in capitalistic funds, mostly from the Ford Foundation, and to reside rather than meet in prestigious Princeton. They were able to represent German literature of the present. How things change for this Group! Those who, at the beginning, took their stance against the representatives of society have themselves become the representatives of society. The pure law of an inner and outer development? A just and proper declaration of power? The great entrance into society? The salt that has become insipid? I know the reasons that have been advanced to justify the change. But I find them singularly unconvincing. At the end of the Princeton meeting, there was a discussion with American colleagues on the "role of the writer in the affluent society," always with the implication that these writers were "opposed" thereto and did not themselves share in the assets of this affluence. It is time for someone to write a new chapter on the "Difficulties in Writing the Truth."

Princeton began apparently in Saulgau (1963) and in Swedish Sigtuna (1964). In Saulgau in Upper Swabia, the television cameras were present for the first time. In Sigtuna, members of the Group were expressly representative. The nature of the meetings changed more and more. From the workshops of Enzensberger's "clique" there now came representatives; the active "assemblage of free spirits" (A 25) developed more and more into a literary stock exchange. Peter Härtling, who had himself once read before the Group, reported on the meeting at Sigtuna: "It is true, they still read their works to one another, still criticize, not less harshly than before, but their chief interest is what people in industry and in other economic enterprises call 'representing' or 'publicity work.' They are 'representatives' of a respected firm, of a holding company (poetry and criticism). . . . Everything is announced: receptions, readings, enraptured interpretation, exclusiveness—even now Scandinavian publishers still ask, when a book is offered them for publication, 'Does the man belong to Group 47?'—'No.'—'I'm sorry ' " (H 204).

What strikes the uninitiated as he pages through the reports of the meetings is how soon the publishers began to make their appearance. Publishers and their representatives were present as early as the spring of 1948—at first Desch and Rowohlt; in the fall, also S. Fischer. Of the meeting at Bad Dürkheim in the spring of 1951, at which the original 20 to 30 participants had already grown to 50, it has been reported: "It must be admitted that they were not all authors in the narrow sense. There were also a number of business men present—readers from publishing houses, radio personnel, journalists; and their presence turned the affair into something like a literary stock exchange. It even happened that a good story was sold, a few hours after it had been read, to three radio stations" (H 59). In the course of the years, the publishing houses whose representatives were most frequently in attendance were Kiepenheuer and Witsch, Luchterhand, Suhrkamp, Augstein from the magazine *Der Spiegel*, Klaus Wagenbach. The most powerful publisher of the Group and the most powerful man in recent "belles lettres" was Siegfried Unseld of the Suhrkamp Publishing Company. A man who knows his power and uses it. When the intellectual center of the Group's work was in Berlin (1966—1967), its publisher was Unseld of Suhrkamp. The groups that formed around Wellershoff in Cologne (at the Kiepenheuer Publishing Company) and around Heissenbüttel in Stuttgart remained on the periphery. How many publishers participated personally or through their representatives in the meetings? At the fall meeting in Berlin in 1965, "Hans Werner Richter requested the publishers who were present to make known their contributions to the prize: twelve raised their hands—at DM 500 [appr. $125.00] per person" (H 207). Mayer-Amery reported after the meeting at Princeton: "To the young writers of today, the Group appears as an established trade union or a peer group that has their future fate in its control" (P 63). Heinrich Böll said in 1965: "The meetings are far from being what they once were, namely 'workshop discussions'; and this change is not to be ascribed to the declining quality of the criticism, which has always fluctuated, but to the quality of the events and their mass publicity. . . . The change occurred at the moment when the German public began to show an interest in German postwar literature. From then on the meetings of the Group became definitely public institutions" (H 393 f.).

It is to be expected in a group that is basically so loose in its organization and so varied in its composition that there would be much coming and going (the coming of the young writers was a matter of survival for the Group). According to all reports and to those who might be expected to know, a so-called "crisis" has been a more or less permanent phenomenon since the early 50s. The crisis was the necessary result of the multiplicity, the coming and going, the differing opinions. It was the "crisis"of vitality. Probably the meeting in the "Powder Mill" in 1967 would not have taken place if there had been no "Berlin nucleus" at the time.[5] According to the Handbook, it consisted of "Hans Werner Richter, Günter Grass, Walter Höllerer, Ernst Schnabel, Hans Magnus Enzensberger, and Reinhard Lettau." "Around this center were grouped a larger circle of young authors, critics, and journalists. Writers like Klaus Roehler and Günter Herburger joined the Group, Klaus Wagenbach founded his one-man publishing company here, critics like Roland H. Wiegenstein and Franz Schonauer settled in Berlin. The literary life of the Group, insofar as it is public, centers around three points: the 'Literarisches Colloquium' on the Wannsee (the leader is Höllerer); the house on Hasensprung Street, where Richter lives; and, finally, the Academy of Arts. . . . The training of the Group (within the Group) takes place here; there are internal forces of authority, but they proceed, if I have judged correctly, not from Hans Werner Richter, the real 'boss' of the Group, but from Günter Grass, who, by reason of his exuberant personality, likes to subordinate certain of the younger writers to himself" (Horst Krüger, critic and member, H 443).

### *Is "Group 47" an Irritant?*

Anyone who is interested in literature today knows the merits of Group 47. Year after year their works have appeared in the literary sections of the great newspapers. It is due chiefly to the efforts of Group 47 that there was a new German postwar literature (a statement that cannot be made with the same assurance about the German film), that there is an effective contemporary literature. They broke down façades, left some halls of the Muses unrebuilt, laid paths through the rubble and, later, through the affluence. They let some old tracks fall into ruin and built many new ones. Because of them, the change, when it occurred, occurred as an awakening. The process by which recent German literature grew into awareness is, in a large measure, identical with the process by which the authors of Group 47 grew into awareness. More strongly than ever before in the history of German literature, the written word was focused on society and society was made aware of the phenomenon of literature. Emphasis was placed on the role of novel, poem, theater in the sphere of social criticism. What Brecht had begun—the achievement for a previously sterile bourgeois and artistic literature, of a social significance and a social objective—Group 47 continued in a new situation. The substance of literary production was made visible in its relationship to publishers and literary critics. It must be admitted, however, that Group 47 was only partially alert to the wrongs of man and of society in this age.

In matters of style, the Group affords much freedom: Eich *and* Heissenbüttel, Celan *and* Enzensberger, Grass *and* Johnson, Walser *and* Becker, Bachmann *and* Wohmann, Rühmkorf *and* Bichsel. But the same freedom was not accorded in matters of political bent. One had to be "left" if one wanted to be and to remain a member of the Group. The distinction between leftist conviction and leftist opportunism was not clearly discernible in every case. The common denominator of leftism was also allowed to affect, more or less expressly, the judgment of literary quality. "The establishment that is most influential in determining what will have success as 'literature' in Germany puts the emphasis not on literary content and form, but on politically tinged and even rather commonplace, nonconformist arrangements. This 'literature' may not conflict thematically with the political sentiment or resentment [of the Group]—a condition that seems to have been fulfilled even when it ignores their demands in matters specifically artistic or esoteric" (Schroers, H 382 f.).

Here and there in the Group some began to confuse quality with inclination. Some, impelled by the vehement urge to presentation that marks the contemporary author, failed to distinguish correctly between the linguistic achievement and the object that it presents. An example: The young Peter Handke wrote after the meeting at Princeton: "I was obliged to hear how much the writer's so-called social *engagement* was measured by the critics of the Group in terms of the objects that he described, rather than of the language in which he described them. That was carried rather far. . . . The so-called 'present,' for instance, was considered to have been treated [in a work] when a computer was described in a story; the so-called 'past' was dealt with when a slide lecture about a trip to Poland was described—and one had only to wait for mention to be made, however casually, of a place called A(uschwitz). And the place was mentioned. . . . How many listeners will be shocked when they hear the mandatory word in this apparently quite harmless travel account! This art of the inconspicuous! And, in fact, Günter Herburger's prose, with its casual mention of the place A, was well received; not, however, because of the particular excellence with which it mentioned the place A, but because 'at last our German present has been treated in the language of a generation.' People admired the casual manner in which the past was mentioned—almost in a subordinate clause. This prose is considered timely not because of its linguistic interest, but because, however naïve the linguistic concept, language is being used without any other consideration to describe the 'German present' frankly and freely" (P 52 f.).[6]

The greatest irritant, however, is probably the Group's unprecedented increase in power. "This power is immense," wrote even the *Lettres Nouvelles* in Paris after the meeting in Princeton. "Just as it sometimes hinders the unfolding of a talent that is already more or less recognized, so it can also further the unknown" (P 67). It lies in the nature of the case that questionable criteria will sometimes be employed in the hindering and furthering. The journalistic and political power of the Group is hardly inferior to its power to determine the literary market (and to write against the "market" of others as well as against the affluent society of others). This power is inherent in the order of magnitude and the literary potentiality of the Group, whose arm reaches almost directly into the friendly publishing firms, radio stations, and literary supplements. Those who once appeared as outsiders have built themselves an immense establishment; an establishment that is—not without a certain self-satisfaction and resentment on their part—nonconformist; an anti-establishment, but nonetheless an establishment. It is no longer possible to believe that they stand on the side of the poor, the free of spirit, the oppressed. Several members have taken their places on the side of the bosses, in the light of publicity, among the prominent, near the mighty.

Group 47 became powerful; in the realms of literature and journalism, it became more powerful than any of its opponents; from a purely quantitative point of view, it held the majority. Then, in 1966, Robert Neumann and Hans Erich Nossack wrote against the Group in the Hamburg monthly magazine *konkret*. At once, Höllerer used a whole issue of his *Sprache im technischen Zeitalter* [Language in a Technical Age] (no. 20, 1966) for a counterattack—fifteen authors against two. A concentrated polemic was directed against Neumann and Nossack under the title *Kunst und Elend der Schmährede* [Art and Poverty of the Diatribe]. Art in the case of Höllerer's authors, poverty in the case of Höllerer's opponents. How simple the denominators have become! Neumann and Nossack wrote very polemically. But fifteen against two, that was hardly fair. One whole issue of a journal directed against three essays that had already had their answer: what could have revealed more clearly the proportions of the existing literary power! Yet they continued to protest against the power of the others. A certain control of the means of publication and communication is, in any event, a problem in today's society. And every control is blind to its own power in more than one eye.

Since Princeton, the Group has had to endure more than just the usual "occupational blindness," the reproach "of insincerity" (Schwab-Felisch, H 407). The decision made before their visit to America that they would not, while they were in the lion's den, protest against the war in Vietnam also belongs to the picture. Richter, Höllerer, and Grass, the leaders of the Group, had not signed the protest against Vietnam drawn up in Hamburg in 1965. Plans had already been made to meet at Princeton in the spring. Non-protest as an opportunistic preliminary achievement for ensuring a friendly reception in the United States?

It would be interesting to trace through the years the change of attitude toward the Group on the part of its prominent individual members, to consider not so much their personal as their objective reasons. Martin Walser, in 1952, when he had just learned of the Group and was suing for its favor, praised Richter and his friends enthusiastically (H 278 ff.). Ten years later, when he was no longer interested—and did not have to be interested because he had made his mark—Walser wrote a very ironic "Letter to a Quite Young Author," in which he glossed for the young literary unknown "the spring and autumn meetings" of the Group and their critics as "annual literary fairs." Again, two years later, in 1964, Walser wrote that the Group—Enzensberger's beloved and much prized "clique"—had "taken on the features of a cartel." This representative of exemplary democracy is in dire need of a "democratic current of air." "It all happened more or less of itself, no ambitious planner worked to make Group 47 what it has now become in the opinion of observers who are to be taken seriously: a monopolistic literary society, something tyrannical, a permanent conspiracy, a famous brand article with a fixed price for even the last buyer" (H 368 ff.). Perhaps there was no "ambitious planner." But there is such a thing as a general trend, an undertow that is inherent in a situation. Why were those who were so keen-sighted about the trends and undertows of their opponents so little aware of their own undertow?

Within the Group, there was a steady process of change: to establishment, to representation, to social pretension, to the "well cultivated suggestion that whatever has literary significance is happening only in Group 47." The Group's role in the "molding of public awareness" began in the late 50s (Schroers, H 383). There developed a harmful relationship between speech and show, work and publicity, reality and image, existence and pose, passivity and demand.

Is the Group approaching its end? After the meeting in Princeton, Richter, in an interview for the Munich newspaper *Abendzeitung* (May 29, 1966), expressed the opinion: "Group 47 was born of the times and will die with the times. I hope that I will know it when the method is out of date." Four weeks previously (April

30, 1966), Joachim Kaiser had written in the *Süddeutsche Zeitung:* "Because the Group is beginning to divide into sub-groups, because those who have achieved success no longer show themselves, because the distinction between commercialism and a meeting devoted to work seems not to have been preserved, for these reasons Group 47 belongs to the institutions for whose end we must prepare ourselves." But also for the reasons indicated earlier. The power of the Group, its establishment, have become too big. For some years now, it has been more like a community of interests than an association of free literary spirits. It would be a totally unprecedented achievement if the authors and publishers who once protested against Springer and self-consciously displayed their undemocratic tendencies were to redemocratize their own Group and with it the distributor stations that belong to it. Democratization would be the option of a free spirit, extinction merely a natural occurrence. Is there a third possibility?

P.S. 1969: *Group* 47 *is dead. It belongs to history.*

# 5

# *Fences and Camps*

*The Writers and the Christians: Reproaches, Reservations, Distrust.*

For a long time—for nearly a thousand years, in fact, and not only in German-speaking lands—Christianity and literature moved toward each other. In Germanic countries, missionaries taught *litterae;* writers used the letters to write as Christians. Within the limits of the knowledge and awareness open to them in a given century, teachers of doctrine and constructors of literature stimulated one another. Even in the Renaissance, when the world was exhibiting unmistakable signs of reorientation and differentiation, both theologians and writers were still teaching a world about which bishops and emperors might indeed contend, but which they were nevertheless ruling together and which they would defend together for some time to come. Since the early phases of the Enlightenment, which witnessed the beginning of the debates between faith and knowledge and the consequent exclusion of the natural sciences from the closed medieval system of integral thought, and even more noticeably since those reflections and procedures that led to the French Revolution, Christian and literary thought have illuminated one another more and more critically, have regarded one another with mutual reservations and finally with mutual reproaches. Since the sixteenth century, each century has been, more markedly than the one before it, a century of emancipation. With the storming of the Bastille began also the storming of the totality that had thus far characterized Christian, metaphysical, late Baroque, and mythical concepts and that had rested upon differences in social classes. In the nineteenth century, the conflict that arose between secular concern for the concrete and a still firmly accepted spiritual teaching was so vehement that all dialogue was cut short, walls were built, and the breach was cemented on all sides.

Today, it is only in the most isolated instances that a practically oriented experience of reality and a spiritually oriented doctrine of salvation are able to dwell together in harmony. Ordinances from above no longer suffice to banish from the world every species of methodical doubt. The bourgeois marketplace, which once linked city hall and church, is today a museum under the protection of the department of public monuments. Men in large cities—and since the period of Naturalism writers have been moving into the cities—pay no attention today to chancery decrees, Sunday proposals, or what amount to spiritual bulk mailings about a salvation that is alleged or wished for, but not dealt with in the stock markets, not exhibited in the newspapers and show windows of their cities. If they must have a utopia, people want one of their own. If they must have a principle of hope, then not one with a Christian label, one that smacks of fad, one that has been whitewashed. What we need is not so much talk about the past as concern for the present, say the writers. Not so much heritage, reflection, possession, but more debate, acquisition, planning. Not the drapes, the clichés, the liturgical vestments hidden behind the heavy doors of Christian sacristies, but the observations of the man in the white laboratory coat, the findings of the social critics, the descriptions of the literary engineer—communication with people who observe. Not the medieval antagonism between God and Satan. Not the world theater of Hofmannsthal, Claudel, or Langgässer. Not the sacral illusion of a Baroque or New Scholastic ideology of knowledge. Not these simple either–or denominators: good and evil, heaven and hell. Not the redemptive psychologizing of the reverts, the metaphysics of the converts, but small recipes for life. A few remedies against the degradation of life, against total manipulation, against fierce criticism.

A few suggestions that have to do with reality. Much criticism —little solace.

In literary matters, too, the Christians have remained outsiders, often enough romantics—romantics of the idea of empire, of church harmony, of a salvation with Gothic, Baroque, New Gothic, or new transcendental vaulting. Despite their manifestos in favor of dialogue, most theologians in office, although they will not admit it, have little use for today's literature. In their eyes, literature is branded with the stigma of a lack of seriousness; its role is too close to that of the actor, the clown, the buffoon. They reproach it for its lack of allegiance. And where such allegiance is found, the Christians in office are inclined to regard it as open or concealed allegiance to the political left, to the opposition, or even to the APO [Ausserparteiliche Organisation, i.e., Communists]; to believe that its sole function is to prepare equal amounts of trouble for government, teachers, patriots, and believing Christians.

For reasons that are readily understandable, most writers have just as little enthusiasm for theology. They see in dogmas and vestments the protective wall, the deception, the muff, the cemented certainty of the ideologist, the well-dressed alibi of the Christian who still brings his business and his God together. Men of letters are even more adamant in refusing to recognize among the theologians a humanly and socially relevant cognitive value than are the theologians with regard to the men of letters. To writers who consider themselves advanced and enlightened—and where would one find a writer under fifty who would claim to be less than that?—to these writers the Christian faith appears to be rather a medieval reliquary than a potential blueprint for ordering the streets of the new age; rather a mythical jelly-fish than an instrument of reason; rather a sleepy loyalty to tradition than a productive unrest directed toward a society of the future.

Social factors are woven into the fabric of distrust. Great lords do as they please within their own camps. Successful men of letters are great lords, too. Those who are not yet successful make great efforts to gain a place among the lords, at the microphones, to be admitted into the camp. Membership in a camp can mean prominence, being allowed to exhibit one's own patent of intellectual nobility in a society of timetables and pills. Under the slogan, "the truth and nothing but the truth," one can write a literature of the camp and a theology of the camp. From time to time, the others build fences. Squint-eyed—those are always the others. Each side claims the press, the prizes, the innocence for its own camp. For these, the papal order—for those, the order of the PEN; not necessarily worn around the neck, but set into the image, its presence implicit even when one is in shirtsleeves and collar.

May the individual venture to formulate reservations, protests, second thoughts, terms for bargaining without being excommunicated by both sides? And yet who, if not the individual, is to reflect on these denominators of friend and foe, to climb over the trenches, to name the fronts? Generalizations are never sharply defined, especially around the edges. They serve, however, to name the matter, to make others aware of tendencies, to light up the areas that lie between, opposite, or even below.

## I. Reservations and Protests of the Writers

"I understand better and better," Heinrich Böll wrote to a young non-Catholic, "that it is becoming constantly harder for your generation, that it causes you almost physical revulsion, to hear the word 'Christian.' "[1] It would be possible, *mutatis mutandis*, to address this sentence to a professional Christian: Do you know that the word 'Christian' is revolting to today's writer? Do you know that this signboard, this systematization, this once-prized label arouses nothing but opposition in today's man of letters? If you do not know it, then your awareness of today's world is obviously not burdened with concepts from history, society, authority, language. You belong to the blissful "haves" who do not want to be disturbed.

For some years now, the writers have been distrustful of the anemia, the pallor, the sublimation, the tendency toward spiritualization, the strictly-for-angels quality of the life preached, taught, and prescribed by Christians. This collection of "thou shalts," "thou shalt nots," "thou musts." This continual limitation of religion to the commandments and of the commandments to the sixth and the observance of the Sunday. Before Nietzsche, Heinrich Heine had already protested against this "Nazarenism." This acid moralism, this "clerical" limitation of consciousness. This unwillingness to admit the physical, sensual, earthly. Some years ago, the American Negro, James Baldwin, wrote: "To be sensual means, I think, to respect and enjoy the vitality of life, life itself; it means to be present in everything that one does, to love from the initial struggle to the breaking of bread." The problem of the presence of truth in all that is alive made its appearance even in the works of Herder and Goethe. "Art... is the... central expression of life," James Joyce has Stephen Daedalus say.[2]

To this category of rarefaction and construction belongs also the Christian campaign for moral literature and clean art, for the kind of novel that might well appear in the Sunday paper, or, at least, for what is not shocking, for what is as harmless as possible. Artists are unmoral, Christians and the still Christian bourgeoisie are moral. This comfortable denominator is far from disappearing. Writers have not forgotten the proceedings against Baudelaire and Flaubert, against Sternheim's *Ulrike* (Leipzig, 1918–1919), against Arthur Schnitzler's *Reigen* [Roundalay] (Berlin, 1922), against Jean Genet's *Notre-Dame-des-Fleurs* (Hamburg, 1962); they have not forgotten the censorship of Wedekind's *Frühlings Erwachen* [Spring's Awakening], of Joyce's *Ulysses*, of D. H. Lawrence's *Lady Chatterley's Lover*, the proceedings against Günter Grass, or *a fortiori* the censorship [formerly] exercised by the Roman Index. More than anything else, perhaps, these were the proceedings and censorship of an authoritarian state, but they were initiated by the denunciations of a more or less Christian bourgeoisie and of the theological guardians of morals. The Christian and bourgeois conscience was far more backward in instigating proceedings against or consigning to the Index those books that were marked by racial discrimination, by anti-Jewish, nationalistic, or militaristic tendencies.

When the writers inquired into the morality of the Christian bourgeoisie who once supported the Kaiser's war (see the protest of the young Brecht), who experienced so few difficulties with regard to Hitler, who protested so softly against the gas chambers, who so early defended the manufacture of atom bombs, and the concepts of rearmament and just war, these inquiring writers were far from receiving a satisfactory answer; they found themselves in an area on which Christian morality had expended too little reflection, of which it had too little knowledge. There is too much formal morality and too little social morality, reported the writers, too much material ethics and too little formal understanding on the part of Christian casuists. Artists and writers defend themselves against the opinion that they are the real bad men of this world, that the Christians are innocent from whatever perspective one may regard them.

In the literature of this century, there has been a very pronounced removal of taboos in sexual matters. But what Christian has addressed himself to this process as to a phenomenon that is also a problem? In 1922, Shane Leslie spoke as a Christian against *Ulysses* [*The Quarterly Review*, no. 473 (Oct. 1922), p. 225]:

> From any Christian point of view this book must be proclaimed anathema, simply because it tries to pour ridicule on the most sacred themes and characters in what has been the religion of Europe for nearly two thousand years.

Mary M. Colum, on the other hand, said ["The Confessions of James Joyce," *The Freeman* 5, no. 123 (July 19, 1922): 452]:

> The alarming thing about "Ulysses" is very different; it is that it shows the amazing inroads that science is making on literature. Mr. Joyce's book is of as much interest as science as it is as literature.... It is as plain as day that a new literary form has appeared, from which the accepted form of the novel has nothing to fear; the novel is as distinct from this form as in his day Samuel Richardson's invention was from the drama.

Valéry Larbaud says with even more emphasis [*La Nouvelle Revue Française* 103 (Apr. 1922): 388 and 408]:

> ... I believe that the boldness and strength with which Joyce portrays...those instincts that are reputed to be the lowest in man come to him ...from the example of the great casuists of the [Jesuit Order].... From these great casuists, Joyce has learned his untroubled coldness and, with regard to the weaknesses of the flesh, the same absence of all human respect.... When one thinks of his rigidity and ...discipline..., one wonders how, from this tremendous repression, there can issue a work so vital, so moving, so human. Obviously, ...the author has never lost sight of the human in his characters, of that mixture of good and evil qualities, of meanness and greatness, of which they are made....

Larbaud, the defender of *Ulysses*, was a writer. Certainly, not everyone is shocked. But the fact that "shocking" literature is sold today in department stores is the fault of the economy more than of the writers. Genet's *Notre-Dame-des-Fleurs* is not harmless. But let the indignant Christian (or bourgeois) read *Ulysses* or *Notre-Dame-des-Fleurs* to the end before he becomes indignant. He will discover that it is no easy task, especially if he attempts any kind of formal reflection. One who presents the sexual in an artistic fashion, spiritualizes it. One who gives form to the brutally sensual, lends it distance—so say the writers. And if this is not the solution to every problem, it is at least supposed to convince the one who does not understand it. In the course of the proceedings against Genet in Hamburg, Buchholz, the general public prosecutor said:

> Earlier literature treated an essential part of human existence—namely the sexual—only indirectly and with obscurity. People shied away from a direct and clear description of these actions. To give one of many possible examples: Richard Wagner's *Walküre*, where, in the first act, the sexual act between brother and sister—incest—is introduced and led toward its climax. . . . This taboo has become less and less operative in the course of literary development. Writers began to picture the sexual, sexual acts, ever more clearly, a direction that has been called erotic realism. The goal of this realism is to give a true picture of the sexual nature. . . . The path of this development, which, as you know, is an international development, is paved with literary trials.[3]

Sartre wrote against an individualistically narrowed concept of morality. The young Brecht protested against a police morality and against the supervisory pretensions of a catechetically narrowed concept of God.[4]

Throughout the centuries, the Christians and their church have maintained a great judiciary title to this world. The title was not always advanced without pose. In a world that is critical of content, a pose belongs to the realm of caricature. In the last decades, the church, the Christians, and their judiciary title have been summoned before the tribunal of the writers. Brecht did it in *St. Joan of the Stockyards*, in *Galileo*, in *The Good Woman of Setzuan;* Max Frisch did it in *Andorra;* Rolf Hochhuth did it in *The Deputy*. In *Andorra*, the girl Barblin asks the priest with his goodly supply of proverbs, who did not hinder the taking of her Jewish brother: "Where were you, Father Benedict, when they came and got our brother like an animal for the slaughter, like an animal for the slaughter, where?" In 1963, when Rolf Hochhuth accused the chief judge of Roman Christianity because he had been silent about the annihilation of the Jews, the accusation echoed around the world. It revealed a widespread latent readiness to see the highest Christian judge accused. Since then, writers have not ceased to direct their questions to the Christian guardians of morality. God's question, "Where were you, Adam?" has become the world's question, "Where were you, Christian?" Where were you, confessor of Christianity, Christian bourgeois, when injustice and public murder were done? Did you recognize evil before it was too late? Did you protest it publicly? Did you separate yourself from it publicly? Or were you one who said "no" only in the privacy of your own room, thus becoming a fellow traveler in public? And what of today? Have you, as a Christian, any concrete answers to the tremendously complicated questions of this age? In all probability, the roles of accuser and accused will be even more completely reversed in the next few years. Writers accuse Christians not because they represent the Gospel, but because they have made the spirit of the Gospel so little visible, because they have prided themselves for so long on their great juridical title and have pretended to know all the answers to all the questions. It is certainly permissible to wonder if every holy spirit is on the side of the "Christians" and every unholy spirit on the side of the writers. The transfer of the role of judge shows a world-wide preoccupation with truth, wakefulness, critical awareness.

From a phrase like "to keep oneself unspotted from this world" (James 1, 27), Christians who think themselves "pious" have been able to derive all kinds of quietistic comfortableness, saltless interiority, lack of interest in the fate of the world, beautiful ideologies about not-soiling-one's-hands in dealing with the world, its lobbies, and its exhaust fumes. They have tried to preserve themselves for the other world and for their otherworldly God. They have not exposed or committed themselves; all too often, they have left the danger zones for others. Christians, say the writers, are to be blamed precisely for this: that they have tried to keep their vests white. They have too often evaded the difficulties, changes, and perplexities of this world that is both a world that is changing and a world that has changed. They have wanted to bake rolls, hand out alms. Holy water for all: for babies, bartenders, department stores, and cannons. Some writers believe that the great leaders of socialism have done more in a hundred years for the good of mankind and the conscience of the world than the whole roster of Christian saints was able to do in a comparable time. Since the French Revolution, these writers point out, human rights and the freedom and equality of the individual have been fought for in arenas that lie outside the church and, in part, even outside Christianity. They see it as an anachronism that the Catholic Church was obliged to concern itself (in Vatican Council II) with questions of general human rights and religious freedom more than a hundred and fifty years after the French Revolution. The development of human freedom and rights has always been intimately connected with morality, with life, and with the spirit of the Gospel.

Today, whether in matters of authority, politics, or religion, the writers themselves want nothing so much as to be free. When asked what he professed, Baldwin answered: "I? Now? Nothing. I'm a writer. I like to act independently." "Writing (like painting, composing, dancing, etc.) is probably one of the few real manifestations of freedom and liberation. Every writer and artist has to cross some borders illegally. . . . Perhaps Catholics, too, will eventually realize," Böll wrote, "that art and freedom are one and the same thing, that they constitute a freedom in which order and form are self-contained; that form is not something 'empty,' but spirit. An author simply appropriates freedom and tries—by ordering and forming it—to share as much of it as possible, which means: to communicate. Everyone is called to participate in this freedom, to take his share of it. The very white white of the nice little average woman and her husband, Mr. Cleanman, is a total nothingness that no longer lets itself be ordered. It is not by accident that the practice of every—*every*—art besmirches him who practices it."[5]

The "little drama of the sound world" that Christians performed for so many centuries, their egoism about salvation, and their tendering of salvation, offended many writers. Because they postulate the existence of a so-called "sound world" and look upon themselves as the possessors of it, Christians, even in this century, have failed to be aware of many problems that exist in this basically unsound world. Too often, they act as though they had acquired the mansions of God as their inheritance, as though these mansions were on a par with the establishments of the rich and the squalid tenements of the slums; as though it were possible to offer salvation like a commodity, complete with salesmen and customer service. In a variety of ways, Paul Valéry, Sartre, Marguerite Duras, Gottfried Benn, Bertolt Brecht, even Rilke, to name only a few, showed their distrust of the "salvation" thus offered and of its representatives. They felt that this salvation was just a stopgap for all that was lacking in the present, a substitute for all that was lacking in existence, a sedative against the awareness of all that was lacking in society. In the proffered salvation, they saw too much prefabrication, too many mechanisms, too much that was synthetic, too little zest, too little reality. "Grace is an eternal rumor," Max Frisch has his Jewish youth Andri say to Pater Benedict, who stands by with his proverbs. "God is nothing but another word for safety," one writer has noted. "The concept of God is valid and useful," Baldwin writes, "only if He can make us greater, freer, and more likable. If God cannot do that, then it is time to get rid of Him."[6] Behind these and similar remarks there is concealed the reproach of Nietzsche, the objection of Marx, the criticism of Kierkegaard, the lament of Kafka.

The reproach against the scientific and political backwardness of Christians is a long-standing reproach of the writers, and one that is still being made. It took the church more than three hundred years to revise—if not so solemnly as it had condemned, then at least implicitly—its judgment about Galileo, about the son who had been possessed of a great new understanding of the world. "They will call the holy church a cesspool of corrupt prejudices," Brecht lets his progressively-minded Urban VIII say in the play about Galileo.[7] The church has taken too long to accept the scientific findings about evolution. Its concepts of the world and of human nature were molded by the world view of antiquity and by a Scholasticism developed on the basis of Platonic and Aristotelian thought. The distrust in matters of science that the critically alert once felt toward the Christian church has remained in force. Today's intellectuals (and the writers include themselves among the intellectuals) have not yet forgotten that no one requires as much time to arrive at a democratic and critically alert political philosophy as do official Christians. Who else served king and emperor as long and as faithfully as did the Christians? Long afterwards, people still linked the concept of Christianity with the concept of a feudal system of government.

Feudalism—that meant order, that meant fidelity to the past, that meant a constant seeking to restore the spiritual unity of throne and altar. How often in the history of Christianity has someone tried to establish God's authority by the use of political means? How often has someone attempted to spread the Gospel by means of ecclesiastical and civil politics? For how long a time were questions of truth decided by the decisions of authority? And in the process, as today's writers are well aware, the eternal was only too often mingled with what was very uneternal. People wanted to keep the Gospel static and authoritarian because they believed that only the static was firm and that the existence of an authoritarian body was the only guarantee of order.

It was much too late when the church finally became aware of the demands of the working classes for their rights. Precisely in their regard, however (where a whole new ordering would have been necessary), the church wanted not "orders" but service through alms, alleviation through the works of mercy. Many theologians will say with justice that these protests are all hardy perennials. But they have not yet been overcome in their practical consequences even today. It is the Christian, and especially the Catholic, form of "provincialism."[8]

The writers are distrustful, too, of the traitorous nearness of so many professional Christians and Christian authorities to the seat of power, to the actual functioning of administrations, organizations, and governments. It seems to them that the spiritual principle, the prophetic aspect of Christianity, has been pushed wilfully into the background. Christian incumbents of office are inclined, wherever possible, to use administrative decrees to dispose of the problems, contradictions, and antinomies of this world. The writers claim that the good Christian, for those in authority, is the one who "functions," who subordinates himself to the apparatus and institutions of church and state. It is quite possible that the unspiritual kind of management indulged in by Christians in office is only a little less dangerous than their spiritual provincialism. The administrators of the Christian sphere would prefer their Christians to possess those virtues that can be administrated, in other words, the secondary virtues of the human sphere. It need hardly be remarked that artists and writers, with their taste for what is vital, with their often prophetic unrest, are basically opposed to any kind of spiritual management.

Among Protestants, the criticism of Christian administrators was linked to a criticism of the Prussian virtues; among Catholics, it was linked to a criticism of "milieu Catholicism." Milieu Catholicism today means this: in the two decades since the end of the war, German Catholicism has remained overwhelmingly dependent upon the concepts of value and virtue that obtain in a relatively closed milieu. It is not the demands of the Christian Gospel as applied to concrete situations that determine Christian behavior and action, but the lazy concepts of the majority, the compulsions of the milieu. The sharpest critics of milieu Catholicism are Heinrich Böll in his novels, Carl Amery in his critical essays. Prussian Protestantism and milieu Catholicism entered into a dangerous alliance of church and state. After the war, they even shared their Christian name with a political party [the CDU = Christian Democratic Union]. This "High C" of politics has been attacked again and again by Günter Grass. Milieu Catholicism and a state church demand conformity of their members. Politically, say the writers, it is impossible to fulfill the promises implicit in the "High C" of an official party title; intellectually, therefore, the claim is a deceptive one.

There is a structural relationship between the type of spirituality that has been referred to as a "closed system" or as the concept of harmony and the type of activity that is not far removed from conformity and mere functioning—the activity of those who proclaim the Gospel because it belongs to their office to do so. Such a procedure tends automatically toward the firm establishment of a system of ideas, toward an ideology. Hermann Broch was concerned about this fact. Albert Camus reacted against it. "Convictions are the best protection against what is vitally true," Max Frisch wrote in his *Diary*. "Convictions as an armor against truth," he wrote in *Die Schwierigen*. Where Christianity prevails, people are too often schooled on convictions. Convictions are something different from a living belief in the Gospel. It is true that a person cannot get along without convictions. But life can become encrusted with convictions if they are formed too early, if they begin even in youth with the study of the Catechism. Then the individual develops a theological system of "nature" and "grace" that takes on the aspect of an inviolable fortress. God and the world, the state and the will of the individual—anyone who wanted to be "of good will" could find a place there. But then came the scientists, then came the critics of the reconciled society. Then came the questions even from within the theological structure. Those who asked the questions were the disturbers of the peace. They were counted among the "wicked."

In his notes on the "epic theater," Brecht criticized the fact that man "is postulated as known" in Aristotelian drama (that is, in classical drama and the drama of the Christian West). In the epic theater, "man is the object of investigation" (W 17, 1009). For a long time now, writers have been consciously concerned with questions about knowledge. No writer today takes as his starting point a cosmos that is whole or a sum for which all the answers can be found. For most writers today, the starting point is that "productive doubt" (Martin Walser) that is more than a matter of method. At the end—and in this they differ from Goethe, Schiller, or Stifter—there are still questions. But Christians and the bourgeoisie want answers, answers that are as direct as possible. "I do not believe," Siegfried Lenz wrote, "that literature has sacrificed any of its function of contributing to the knowability of man in time, or at least of determining the possibility of such knowability. It is less concerned with solving the questions of existence than with asking them."[9]

As an example of the concept of harmony, the writers' "party" might well cite a Catholic monthly journal of the year 1931. Under the title "Rational World Picture of a Catholic Writer," there appears a review of Leopold Andrian's work *Die Ständeordnung des Alls* [The Hierarchical Order of the Universe] (Munich, 1930). The review begins as follows: "In our troubled times, this important subtitle (i.e., the title of the article) will catch the attention of everyone who has either preserved or regained for himself a sense of the unity that is present in the world plan and of the challenge that can be understood and deduced from it for the oneness of our own essence, our desires, our actions. Briefly, this book has something to say to everyone whose concept of time and whose feeling about the world is not mired in and fulfilled by the worship of the moment. Indeed, I cannot think of a single soul among men anywhere in the world in whom the basic thought of this work would not find fruitful soil, whether it produced jubilant agreement or a wistful

'Thus it should be'. . . . Indeed, it is beauty that has so impressed Andrian; in the beauty of the universe he recognizes the will of God and in terms of this beauty he seeks to explain the act of creation. The thought that each man . . . is able to see and to experience; that this road leads ever higher to that place where beauty appears as world-wide *harmony* and even beyond to the steps of God's throne, where beauty shines in the clear light of *order:* the thought that precisely this road can be the road to God for the men of our age is truly a great thought and—though it is as old as time—a thought for today because it points with vigor and courage into tomorrow. And since a poet has written the book, this great thought was entrusted to pure senses and hands."[10] The overtones of a new romanticism and an old Platonism are unmistakable. It is astounding to come upon this smooth ordering of the universe only two years before Hitler's rise to power. "Brave old world," beautiful Catholic world, might have been the ironic title of Huxley's novel. Certainly no one will say such things again with the superb confidence that was possible in 1931. But in many Christian judgments about society in general and about literature and art in particular, the uncritical residue of thinking based on such ideas of harmony, splendor, and reflected glory is to be detected even today. Even in this day and age, it can still happen that the person who ventures to scratch this theologically lacquered harmony, who questions the value of this eternal wholeness can be publicly denounced. How often this concept of harmony has been attacked in literature. The young Friedrich Schlegel began the attack after the events of the French Revolution. The attacks of Heinrich Heine and Georg Büchner in the first half of the nineteenth century were carried out with more vigor. Kafka and Sartre, Brecht and Max Frisch, Heinrich Böll and Günter Grass have also, each in his own way, attacked and criticized this concept. The writers are irritated because Christians have, for centuries, been unwilling to see the great and small grotesqueries, the discrepancies, the dissonances, the static ledgers of life. Because they subscribed to a mode of thinking that smoothed away all wrinkles, people in the Christian camp were able to pay homage to the concept that literature should "beautify" life, should bring man "consolation." But the writers constantly refuse to join the Christian "beautification" league or to support the Christian "consolation market" (the harsh word is Rilke's). "Consolation in literature is only too often a cheap consolation," Dürrenmatt wrote in his comments on the theater. "It is certainly more honest to keep the human point of view." Point 19 about *Die Physiker* [The Physicists] reads: "Reality appears in paradoxes." Point 20: "Whoever confronts paradoxes exposes himself to reality." Max Frisch noted in his *Diary:* "The Pietà of Michelangelo. (From the Capella Barbarini in Santa Rosalia in Palestrina.) Here is an end to beauty; the weight of the corpse with its knees bent inward and its arms hanging, the hideousness of the body that belongs now only to heaviness, the anxiety lest its accidental movements may become suddenly grotesque, laughable like those of a marionette. . . . The supra-beautiful: the bodies that they loaded onto trucks and threw into a lime-pit, it is possible to remember them without being shocked at one's enjoyment of art; they, too, are contained here. They are not mocked and betrayed by an art that is concerned only with beauty. Only when the hideous is also present does there begin the possibility of a redemption that is more than a premature harmony."[11]

The question of salvation is by no means omitted from present-day literature. But it has been coming for some time now from a quite different source than when it was asked by the Christians: from those who suffer anxiety, from the night, from prison, from the cell, from the inability to communicate. It comes as a radical question about existence and language in the case of Kafka and Sartre, as a question about the good society in the case of Brecht, as a question of meaning in the face of the absurd in the case of Camus, as a question of meaning in the gestically lamenting figure of the grotesque and the absurd in the case of Samuel Beckett. It is not a literature of happiness. Nor is it the successor of an idealistic classicism or a literature of the "garden house." In the literature of classicism, there was a question of a life that had succeeded, of a life that was basically happy. Classical literature attempted (especially the classical German psychological novel) to make man more comprehensible in a human fashion. Such an optimistic and idealistic literature could afford to be comparative. Even providing that life is already present and guaranteed, today's literature, as everyone knows, is not concerned with the better or happier life. Today's literature is a never-ending criticism of a society that hinders life or makes it impossible. Its only concern is to discover life, to make it credible even as a possibility in a society that is so tightly administered, in a world of technocratic and bureaucratic dissensions, of such aggressive confusion. This literature is about assent to a life that is being questioned from right and left, that is encompassed by a paralyzing greed for more (more progress, more possessions, more comfort, more pleasure, more power). It is because life itself has become so problematical that contemporary literature has become so aggressive, as aggressive as the speeches of the prophets of old. Amid the violence, there is revealed, in contrast to the more contemplative literature of an earlier age, the operative and gestic literature of a Homo Faber, of a Job protesting and helpless as a late-born Prometheus. Because the negative is so ruthlessly bent on demonstration, there arises the urge to create happenings. Obviously nothing now but the loud, the demonstrated, the massive "event" can reach the reader who has been surfeited with a flood of irritants or the spectator who has become insensible. This literature of existence, of the operative, of the caricatural, of the grotesque and the concrete is primarily a literature of the intensive, a literature of injured man, a literature in search of society. Christian theology and its message were too long a matter of the extensive, of the society postulated as functionable, of the basically intact existence that was in need of nothing but exhortation and absolution. The foil to such a literature and such an interpretation of what it means to be a Christian is not far to seek. It is a matter of structure.

Questions of form and language dart in and out amid the so-called reproaches and contradictions. The writers find fault because Christians and theologians are so little able to recognize aesthetic form. Christians and theologians are too little aware that linguistic and formal achievements are also moral achievements. On the part of the writers, there is first of all a morality of knowledge, of non-evasion and of a firm stance in the face of what can be experienced. Then there is a morality of language and form. A sentence that describes, a work that is well constructed, an image that is precise, a metaphor that reveals, a line that leads beyond itself into the sphere of knowledge—all these are human and moral achievements, a creative addition to truth, reality, possibility, to everything in this world that has not yet become expression. Ingeborg Bachmann, in her lectures on poetry in Frankfurt (1960), designated precisely this morality of knowledge and form as a stimulus for the spirit. Christians are to be blamed for their too one-sided reading of content alone. They have difficulties wherever content appears in and as form, wherever morality appears as form. They are too little aware of the process of truth, the process of spiritualization, of the humanizing that has taken place through the process of giving expression and form. This world finds itself when and where it finds expression in word. Perhaps it does not find its way to the communion rail in church. But something in this world communicates in the word.

Professional Christians know little of the strain of speech, scarcely know what effort it costs to find the right word or the creative word. For this reason, they fail to observe how little speech is involved in their daily activities, in their churchly, theological, catechetical, homiletic, even liturgical activities. The pastoral letters of bishops are often painfully lacking where language is concerned. Therefore it becomes clear that language is not something that can be taken for granted, but something that must be achieved; that language communicates or does not communicate. In Martin Walser's *Halbzeit* [Half-time], Anselm's wife Alissa writes in her diary: "With Lissa to church. Couldn't pray. The compulsion to think of Anselm is stronger. Then I can think in my own words. The solemn official language in church sounded alien. The vocabulary of applied art. Air that is pure sultriness. Do the pious believe that God hears them only when they pray, that He has no notion of the words that they are otherwise thinking and saying? It is impossible to believe that the pastor has experienced what he tells about in his sermon. My life can no longer be brought within the scope of the language of prayers. I can't distort myself so. I inherited God in these formulas, but now I am losing Him because of them. People make Him into a magic privy councilor whose eccentric mode of speech they accept because God belongs to yesterday anyway."

In *Die Physiker*, Dürrenmatt treats with irony the prating speech of the missionary Rose, whose second marriage, to the former wife of Möbius, had added the three Möbius children to his own six. The missionary Rose says to Möbius in the insane asylum: "I have them all locked in my heart, Mr. Möbius, all three of them. God will help us as the Psalm says: The Lord is my shepherd, I shall want for nothing."[12] "Light as soap bubbles," Günter Grass calls the liturgical formulas of blessing in "Hochwürden Gusewskis gespitzter Mund" [Reverend Gusewski's Pursed Lips] in *Katz und Maus* [Cat and Mouse]. The Christians will have to become more aware of their poverty where language is concerned. They will have to notice that failure to speak may indicate not just lack, but even guilt. They will have to assume the burden of a language that is not paternalistic. What Günter Eich admitted of himself is true of many writers: "It is only when I begin to write that many things achieve reality for me. This reality is not my prerequisite, but my goal. I must first construct it. I am a writer, and that is not just a profession, but the decision to see the world as language. The real language seems to me to be the one in which word and thing coincide. We have to translate from this language that is found all around us, but that is still not present to us. We translate without having the original text. The most successful translation is the one that comes closest to the original and that achieves the highest degree of reality."[13] One of the greatest contrasts between writers and theologians becomes apparent in these words.

The preceding pages make it clear that the reproaches and reservations of writers toward Christians are of various kinds. Some of them are due to commitments and viewpoints that belong specifically to writers. Others are due to factors that belong more generally to mankind. But all of them are advanced by men who observe with critical alertness from their position on the edge of Christianity and of a society that considers itself Christian. This fact proves what we already know—that most writers today do not live in the sphere of professional Christianity or of any churchly orthodoxy. It proves, too, that the writers, in their own way, are sons and citizens of their age; that they help the age to find awareness in word. The writers are men. In their works, they have formulated, given literary expression to, and spread a series of reproaches against the image and the concrete form assumed by Christianity today. Literature formulates what is human. What is human in any age gives form to literature. The Christian must prove himself on what is human.

## II. Reproaches and Misgivings of the Christians

Christians also reflect upon man. Christians also suffer in this world. Christians can communicate to the writers something that the writers either do not see at all or see with limited vision. Many writers act as though they were still dealing with the Christians of a prescientific age. They behave as though they have to defend themselves against a Christian rearguard, against those who are too lazy or too apathetic to think. But what if there are some Christians who are not simply members of an association of watchmen and doorkeepers, who no longer play the "little drama of the sound world," but who, for some time now, have been engaging with extraordinarily subtle awareness in the conflicts between contemporary society and the salvation promised, though not unreservedly, by Christ?

The word "Christian" in this context refers to those who are critically alert, who are conscious, who ask questions, who reflect; in many instances, this means the theologians, those whose profession it is to think on Christian matters, to speak on Christian matters, to write on Christian matters. Only those who are alert can enter into dialogue with the writers. In their own interest, some have erected the equation "intelligent writers—stupid Christians." It is unfair, uninteresting. Eventually, some writers will have to notice and admit that some Christians are critically alert, that their alertness is not inferior to that of the writers, that their sincerity will not be put to shame by the sincerity of the writers. What distinguishes the alertness and sincerity of these Christians is primarily the object upon which they are expended. The particular point of view from which Christians contemplate reality, the perspective from which they must interpret the *condition humaine*, is that of the Word of God spoken unto this world and historically manifested in it. A manifestation at once exacting and hidden, and one that has been exposed to trials and eclipses in the whole course of human history. It is conceivable that Christians, by reason of their particular perspective, will perceive much that writers as writers either do not perceive or perceive in a different manner. If they want to be fair, writers must admit that Christians also have a claim to that knowledge on which writers place so much emphasis. Otherwise, there can be no dialogue. Without this prerequisite, the other—in this case, the Christian—will not be admitted as a partner in the dialogue.

In the first place, Christians can simply reverse many of the arguments that are being advanced by the writers. What the writers say about professional Christians and theologians—that they are uneducated, underdeveloped, backward in matters of literature—the educated Christian can say with equal justice about the writers when theology is under discussion. What writer from Berlin to Cologne or Munich can claim to have read Karl Barth, Bultmann, Gogarten, Bonhoeffer, Tillich, Karl Rahner, Moltmann, Pannenberg, Hans Küng, or Johannes B. Metz? To have read not all, but even one of these theologians who are giving so much intensive thought to what Jesus Christ said about salvation or to the condition and expectation of this world. Many writers are not just uninterested in Christian theology; they are ignorant of it. What they once learned under compulsion from their childhood catechism; the image that is both too brightly and too dimly lighted by their emotions; their political concept of Christians—they confuse all these with the reality of being Christian. They are as little ready to inaugurate joint discussions or dialogues with the Christians as the Christians are to do so with them. In recent years, important writers have been invited again and again by student chaplains and Christian Academies to hold discussions or to give lectures; they have been invited on time; they have been given sufficient choice of date; they have been offered a fitting honorarium. Yet, in many cases, the important writers have not accepted these invitations. Only because it was difficult to decide on a date? Or was there also a problem of willingness, of appearances to be kept up, of fear about their image? Why do professional nonconformists so seldom engage in dialogue with those whom they have labeled wicked conformists? Perhaps the dialogue would be too self-revealing? Perhaps they would destroy a few prejudices? Perhaps their image would acquire a black mark in their own camp? Where, in all this, is their much-prized small freedom?

There are writers who emphasize their lack of reservations so strongly that one asks oneself if these proclaimers of their own open-mindedness are not speaking in a merely popular sense. Often enough, their tone reveals an emotionality that can be explained only as resentment. Apparently their so-called impartiality or open-mindedness means: I do not believe in your (and your and your) denominator. I have my own. You wear glasses. I do not. At least, I don't wear your glasses. When he was asked what he thought of Christianity, the writer Arno Schmidt answered: "It's high time to let Christianity know what an impartial person thinks about it: today, with synods and Godseekers on every horizon, shadowy figures with scholastically wrinkled foreheads in the clouds, infallible, disapproving, aged. . . ." As an explanation of his "no," of his "not so very much," Schmidt mentions "the questionableness of the institution's primary document (that is, the Bible), the (for me) unsatisfactory person of Jesus of Nazareth. Finally, contemplation of the effects of Christianity in its sphere of influence." He rejects the Bible because it has, "by even the most lenient reckoning, 50,000 textual variations" and is a book "in which there is no human understanding." Does he know that no book of comparable age and a comparable number of parts has been transmitted with any greater accuracy? To be logical, Schmidt should have rejected every literary text that has been handed down in several codices. And to say that there is "no human understanding" in the Bible is more than just a lack of understanding of the textual history; it is pure polemics. As his third argument, Schmidt flatly denies that "Christianity has increased the amount of the good, the true, and the beautiful in the world." His reason: "How could painting have flourished when iconoclastic squabbles so often took the ground completely from under its feet?" But painting, as we know, did flourish to an extraordinary degree.

About the person of Christ, Schmidt says:

> The person of this man, whose name has been adopted by 30% of mankind, does not satisfy me!—What would we say today if a young man came from some dwarf state or other; from one of the ever present and not just 'economically underveloped' regions of the East; able to speak none of the languages of culture; totally unacquainted with all that science, art, technology, and even eariler religions have achieved throughout the millenia—and such a one stood before us with the prepos-terous words: 'I am the way; and the truth; and the life'? First of all, we would have to call in an interpreter and have him carefully translate the barbaric dialect for us—would we not advise him, half in jest, half in perplexity: 'Young man: first live and learn: and come back

in thirty years!'? But this is precisely the case of Jesus of Nazareth. . . . For me, anything that such a man affirms is *a priori* not discussable![14]

The critical reader will ask himself how "impartial" the writer is for whom some things are "not discussable," how such noncomprehension and miscomprehension are possible. What we have here is the direct admission of a writer. But when this misunderstanding of what is Christian enters into a literary work, into the actions that it presents, into the words and images, when it inserts itself into a clearcut observation of daily life and of language, then it appears not directly, but through the mirror and fragments of reality, through the suggestion that has been built into the sentences. Then a literature is born in which threads of varying quality are woven together, in which both clear vision and a vision that is clouded or even vitiated dictate the words. There are writers today who regard Christians with clouded or vitiated vision. Should such writers be surprised if Christians regard them with reservations? As in the case of Arno Schmidt, they have first rejected the Christians and all that they stand for.

Let us assume for the moment that a Christian is reading the following poem by Eberhard Meckel, which appeared in *Die Zeit* on July 26, 1968.

*Prayer*
Great God even of Biafra,
kind God of all children,
for whom it is Your will
that they come to You—
Send more Migs so they can come faster,
send more weapons from Skoda, many more,
from Oerlikon, too—Vickers, Mausers, FNs,
to shorten their way
to You.

Send a heaven full.
From all Your heavens
choose one of napalm
so that everything will burn more quickly,
the light coconut huts,
the grass savannas,

the secret beaten tracks
of powdered milk supplies
for the unauthorized supplies of the Ibos.
We make You an offering, too,
of pure oil from Onitsha
for Your eternal flame.[15]

Is the poem to be regarded as provocation, misunderstanding, blasphemy? As provocation based on misunderstanding? At whom is it directed? Against all who murder and support murder, especially the bourgeoisie with Christian portfolios who offer "oil from Onitsha" for God's "eternal flame"? If so, then are there actually any "Christian" actionists who believe as primitively as the text presumes in their "great God of Biafra"? Must it not appear blasphemous or stupid to ears trained in theology that it has to be "God" Who was responsible for the horrors in Biafra, for the delivery of arms from West and East, for the civil war in Africa? If the text is meant as a satire, as a sarcastic complaint, at whom is it directed? Who is being addressed? Where is he? Did anyone who participated in the Nigerian civil war really believe that he was acting in the name of God? Was the mantle of Christianity present at all? Did any of the participants or the representatives of special interests think of appealing to "God" in order to achieve genocide more quickly? Was "God" supposed to end the war that He had not begun? Was not that completely and solely a matter for men? Why use the notion of "prayer" to decorate a satire that fits no one? For arguments and insinuations that proceed from false assumptions? So that the Christians and their God may once again be put in a bad light? So that there will once again be something provocative in the newspapers? So that the servants of the Christian God may once again be made the scapegoats, if possible the only scapegoats of this world? So that non-Christians can prove their superior morality?

Provocation as jam for the feuilletons? As an injection of cocaine in the evening? As a stimulating drink for the weekend? The word of the writers as cocktail or moral? Or perhaps the cocktail as moral? Why did not the author of the text take the trouble to find out who were the real addressees, those really concerned, the real motives of the African war? Why the emotionally laden stab in the dark? Where, in this instance, is the writer's critical awareness? Is he not taking the easy way of winning concurrence from those who think as he does, the applause of the gallery? Among writers, too, there are ideological prejudices, ideological trimmings, ideological cunning, ideological partiality.

Even among those writers who consider themselves Christians, there is an astounding lack of knowledge, a distressing retardation where the theological discussion and knowledge of today are concerned. A personal comment may be in order. In the late autumn of 1967, a writer who considers himself a Christian complained about the backwardness of religious knowledge, beginning with the Catechism. But at that time the "Dutch Catechism" was already a year old and had been much discussed in the public press. There was even a complete German translation of it—the so-called "Study Edition." I asked the complaining writer if he had heard about the Dutch Catechism for adults; if he knew that it took questioning mankind as its starting point, accepted modern man's experience of reality as a precedent condition, and treated it as a difficult problem; that it made no claim to solve all of man's problems. The critic of Christian awareness said "no." He was totally unaware of the fact that he was raising complaints that were no longer pertinent. He did not know that his "Christian" awareness lagged far behind the differentiated awareness of today's theologians. He was still talking as though theologians were backwoodsmen or provincial journeymen, as though there were no leaven and almost no Spirit in the church. Are there not comfortable denominators, labels, files, clichés even among writers? Many a Christian must often wish that many a writer would evince less resentment and more knowledge, a more critical procedure in forming his judgments.

Which of today's writers would be able to give an account of the very subtle deliberations in the realm of theology? Of the way in which Christians understand faith, church, eschatology? Of that area that used to be called "original sin" and that is not dissimilar to what Marxists call "alienation"? Of the changes that have occurred in the theological understanding of the world, even to the evolution of a theology of politics? Of the new deliberations about the theology of the sacraments, about the principles of hermeneutics, about the historical and social factors that condition every assumption, about exegetical questions even including the resurrection of Christ? At least the writers should not act, either implicitly or explicitly, as if there were no critically aware thinking in the realm of theology. What writer could say or demonstrate today what "salvation" really means? Salvation as the promise and testament of that Man of Nazareth Whose involvement in the debates of His own time was so intense, yet so tragic? Certainly salvation has many names. Horizons, perspectives, partial horizons. Kafka's K. and Beckett's tramp, the Marxist utopians and the Western social engineers, those who are obsessed with their own individuality, those who inquire only about their own identity (Max Frisch's principal characters), those who dream about a paradise lost or to be regained, those who struggle for a "last great freedom" (Zwerenz)—all of them are looking with fascination at one or other aspect or sector of salvation. At sectors: that means that they act as heretics do (haireo: I take out for myself). Despite their protestations of being dynamic and vital, the writers are, in their own way, preoccupied with fixations—fixations about direction, scope, denominator, sector. Should they be surprised that the Christian, led by Christ, sees a greater horizon of truth and reality, that his gaze encompasses other levels of freedom, of life, of ways of encountering himself and others?

The writers' awareness of truth and their relation to truth often seem to critical Christians to be susceptible of criticism. Writers are inclined to equate truthfulness with truth, personal integrity with the way the world itself is constituted. They are too little aware of the discrepancy between subjective integrity and objective truth, between exact description of an episode, of a kind of awareness, of an experience and that objective claim to truth that lies at the base of the episode, the awareness, the experience—the perspective of understanding. In Thomas Mann's *Joseph*-novel, for instance, the Christian is constantly confronted with the question as to whether there is a harder and more demanding truth than that which is presented by the "epic whisperer of the imperfect," than that which is known to the psychologizing painter of history and teller of stories. What happens to the truth when a writer, for instance a Marxist, confesses a social philosophy that he makes the sole criterion of truth itself, about which he affirms that it (at least basically) solves all questions? What happens, on the other hand, if a writer simply wants to exclude the theoretical, empirical side of truth and considers his "moral" obligation to recognizable truth satisfied when he poses the question: "How can I remain true to myself in my writing? How do I go about making my truth acceptable? How do I make it effective?"[16] How are we to evaluate truth in the case of those writers who loudly proclaim their promise of salvation, but who afterwards appear to have offered nothing but a mixture of longing, partial knowledge, pathos, social criticism, and snatches of reality couched in suggestive literary form? For example: the Young Germans in the 30s and 40s of the nineteenth century; the Expressionists in the second and third decades of the twentieth century. In point of fact, then, the truth of the writers is contestable, is often susceptible to criticism even by those who today are counted among the scapegoats of this world, the Christians. Has not every generation of writers proved to the preceding generation that it had considered its own perceptual and conceptual systems absolute, that it—in its own way and except for a few really great writers—had adapted itself to the trends, the spirit, the fashion of its times? And what of the vanity that feigns truth?

What are we to think of the denominators of friend and foe as used by many writers and literary critics? Of the manipulations in the camp of the publishers and publicists? What are we to think of the moral denominators in the written word? Are these denominators and labels really so impartial? Is it really so impartial to demand emancipation but merely to tolerate enlightenment as a goal? Are not the labels "good" and "bad" often assigned rather one-sidedly? Is truth to be found only in one's own camp?

It is not easy to explain away the reproach that a political party is making use of the "High C." But the addition of the word "Christian" must first be understood properly, that is, in historical context. It was the experience of the Hitler years and the collapse in 1945 that made the Christians of both confessions see the value of a united political action. This desire for a joint action of the two confessions in forming the political will led to the adoption of the title "Union"—the union of the members of the two Christian confessions in a new democracy: CDU (Christliche Demokratische Union=Christian Democratic Union). Even if the word "Christian" is viewed theologically and ethically, and even if we are prepared, like Günter Grass, to narrow the concept of Christian to ethics and even to the ethics of the Sermon on the Mount, it is still clear that the Party cannot fulfill all that it implicitly promises by calling itself "Christian." For the politician, there are, however, practical considerations that must be taken into account. A large and well-established political party is no more able to change its name without suffering considerable loss than is a large and well-established business firm. There is no intention, here, of defending the "High C," but of doing justice to names and things.

What we have called milieu Catholicism will not be overcome between today and tomorrow. From the theological point of view, something has already been done—from the Dutch Catechism for adults to the new theological questions about the Christian's awareness of God and his understanding of the church and of himself—to take the water out of the mills of milieu Catholicism. But the overcoming of milieu Catholicism is also a matter for bishops and clubs, and a question of better knowledge and enlightenment for the broad masses of people within the church.

One group of protests that the writers raise against Christianity and its professional Christians is not only admitted by numerous professional Christians, but even shared by them. The current regression in interiority; the anemia; the paleness of the Christian element; the absence of all understanding for the crooked lines of what is alive, for what is not schematized, for what is daring and dangerous; the residue of moralizing; a morality that is too onesidedly concerned with material things, casuistry, self-righteousness; the attempts that persist into the twentieth century to create a harmonious world view; the erection of a sacral life alongside of and above the difficult life of everyday—all that has been under discussion within the church for a long time, often even with much professional understanding. The lack of dialogue in the religious sphere is only too well known to alert Christians. Some theologians would ask, however, if it is not the feeling for what is alive, for the achievements and directions of life, for spontaneity and wholeness, that has been sacrificed by the intellectual writers, the writers of the absurd, of the extremely paradoxical, of schizoid sex. Within the Christian, and especially the Catholic, sphere, there used to be that comfortable truth that is peculiar to the closed system as such. Today, among writers, there is also a comfort that is derived from what is open, a tendency not to let oneself be pinned down, an intellectualizing and artificial irony that relativizes nearly everything, poses questions about everything, but avoids all answers and the consequences of answers. Are they sufficiently aware that man cannot live by skepticism and questions alone?

Christians might ask if the writers, with their overemphasis on social morality, are not also being one-sided when they refuse to recognize the existence of personal and existential guilt. Brecht provides what is probably the most obvious example of the omission of every form of alienation and determinable guilt except those rooted in society; in this respect, he is the extreme opposite of Strindberg and Ibsen as well as of Kafka, of Kleist as well as of T. S. Eliot. Critical Christians might also ask if the radical removal of taboos is in itself such a great bringer of blessings, if it alone can inaugurate the great freedom. They might ask further if the writers' rejection of the "image of man" that earlier generations held sacred, if their constant emphasis on what we have lost and their insistent reminders of the *negativa* of our race, if this total criticism of all that we have will prove sufficient in the long run, or if the tendency to total criticism and the aggressiveness of the tone are not already proving a boomerang to the critics. Does not a tendency to total parody, total irony, and total constructionism on the part of the writers betray the same lack of comprehension for the organic, the same preponderance of the cerebral and the artificial that they complain about, on the one hand, as a lack of nature in this world and that they are themselves guilty of cultivating on the other hand? Is there not, on the part of the writers, a negativistic reveling, a luxuriating aggressiveness, a narcissistic self-righteousness? Does not life defend itself from time to time against the caricatures and destructiveness of the writers? Have not today's writers rather comfortable procedures for hacking words and contexts to pieces? Does not life still have laws that stop short of constructionism and beyond manipulation? Do the writers reveal only the manipulations of others? Do they themselves never take part in the manipulation of the word, in manipulation in their dealings with their fellow men?

Generations or professions that set little value on historical tradition and regard what has been transmitted from the past with the superficial interest that snobs reserve for what is contemporary find it relatively easy to accept every new hypothesis or knowledge in the name of an often only alleged truth. They want to belong to the present, but without having to pay a great price. They do not ask about the possibility of union between yesterday and today, but of union between today and the day before yesterday. They have sacrificed the tension of historical continuity. They relegate the concept of a totality of faith and knowledge to the storage rooms of the museum. They can no longer endure the conflict of history and totality. They are hardly aware of any other criteria than their own current ones and those of their contemporaries. It is harder for Christians. Galileo in the seventeenth century, Darwin in the nineteenth, polygenesis in the twentieth, even Marx and Freud—each presented as the message of the age par excellence—create problems for them.

The aged Goethe knew about the tension between the present and tradition. "We are always doing battle with tradition," he wrote in his *Maximen und Reflexionen* [*Maxims and Reflections*], "and the demand that we should experience the present on our own authority is, at the same time, a challenge to a dangerous conflict. And yet the man who has been gifted with creativity feels the call to fight personally in this double battle that is made harder not easier by the advance of science."

What did Thomas Mann have to say, in a context that is admittedly suspect, about men of letters, about those painfully up-to-the-moment writers with their distorted views of civilization? "A man of letters, then, is one who always knows exactly: 'What we ought to do now is . . . ,' and can always do it, too. Everything else is just commentary. The man of letters, you see, does not *be*, he only judges—a cheerful, enviable lot, as I have often discovered. For how easy it is for one who only has to judge to leap into the boat, never to miss his connection, always to be found arm in arm with the latest ideas of Youth."[17] Despite the unequivocal tendency that Thomas Mann revealed in *Betrachtungen eines Unpolitischen* (he revised them later), something emerges here that belongs all too often to the phenomenon of literature. Not all writers are men of letters in the way that Thomas Mann describes them here. But in the literary exchanges, a similar dilettantism in literature is being offered and sold even today.

According to the writers, the Christians in our industrial age have concerned themselves neither intensively nor extensively with the needs of the working class. The Christians have misunderstood the revolutionary self-help of the proletariat. The Christians, who are aware of their guilt in this respect, nevertheless point to the fact that numerous writers in those decades (and not just Thomas Mann) either took their stand totally on the side of the bourgeoisie or had no thought at all to spare for the needs of the proletariat. They (and not just Rilke and George) were preoccupied with their own individuality, their own artistry and form. They had withdrawn from society and entrenched themselves in esoteric solitude. For the rest, there were a few Socialists among the writers as there were among the Christians. It is not possible to see much advantage for one side or the other in today's mutual counting of minus points. In the years under discussion, there was unquestionably more bourgeois than Socialist literature.

Not only the Christians but even the writers had buried their existence in the subjectivity of the individual, the interiority of the beautiful, in subtle self-gratification and narcissism, in pleasure formed to their own specifications. It is well known that the Christian Kierkegaard reproached the writers of his century because their existence was so lacking. Today, many writers act as though the greatest sins were contemplation and interiority. Wherever one turns today, one finds that only action, demonstration, agitation, noise are allowed to count for anything. Some writers seem to know nothing at all about the vital tension between interior and exterior, between knowing and acting, speech and silence, action and contemplation. The present problem of the writers—and Christians are beginning to know it too—is not that they set too high a value on interiority, but that they set no value at all on it, that they are consumed by an all-absorbing drive toward politics, political journalism, anything that attracts attention and makes noise. Writers regard themselves as the salt and leaven of our society. How can they continue to fulfill this function if they are themselves yielding to the superficial, the journalistic, to the same fleeting awareness that they criticize in their readers?

A third group of problems is more or less latent in the irremovable tensions between literature and Gospel, between writer and Christian. The Gospel bears witness to an event and proclaims a message. Both event and message are on the same level, and it is not the level of literature. Today, literature speaks entirely in its own name. But the Christian stands under the aegis and name of another, of that Man Who bore witness to Himself as the incarnate Son of God and from Whose messianic function the Christian derives his name. The Christian cannot simply overlook the matter of God. For on the Christian level there is that stumbling block of which Paul once spoke—the stumbling block of what they claim, the stumbling block of salvation. Today, the people of this world are again seeking first in other places (than in Christ) for "signs" and "wisdom." The message of the Crucified One is the one "stumbling block," the one "foolishness" (1 Cor. 1, 22 f.). The Christian must insist that this world be understood not only as a world that can be constructed and organized, but as a world created by God, fallen into sin, and redeemed by Christ, as a world that is eminently transparent. He cannot say, as can the writer, that he understands the world primarily as speech—unless he is referring to the word of revelation and its presence or absence in the speech to which he is referring. But that is what the writer does not do. In ever new attempts and beginnings, the writer searches for the "text" of the world. The Christian, on the other hand, must believe that he already possesses a good part of this text, the "original text" of the Biblical revelation, that his task is to understand, accept, realize, and spread it. This "original text" is no comfortable possession. A man must devote his whole life to the process of learning it, of appropriating or not appropriating it. Today's writer often takes the *tabula rasa* as his starting point. He demolishes all content (finds them partially demolished). In his statements about human existence, he doubts everything except his own experience of reality. He is less prepared than ever before to accept the interpretation of another. The Christian, on the contrary, must expose himself to the experience of others and to their witness. These others are the men and women who once knew Christ personally and who, before and afterwards, shared in the spirit that is prophetic and that bears witness. Naturally the Christian was in danger of taking this "original text" too naïvely, of not regarding the history of its origin and its literary genres. He was afraid that he might lose the inexorableness of the matter if he turned the text into literature. Today, the Christian is in danger again, this time of equating the "original text" of his Scriptures with the "original text" of the world, of reality, spirit, and language as such, of looking only at his own text and of setting a low value on those texts of human understanding that have arisen in other places and other times, of ignoring them or of wanting to treat them as merely primitive. He has learned, in the meantime, that the Bible does not contain all words and answers, that the growing reality that man has altered and for which he is responsible creates new texts. Fundamentally, however, he still sees the Bible, the "original text," as belonging on a different level from that of any text that came later, of any literary word that is totally of this world. But in whatever sphere he must conclude that his "original text" does not provide answers, in that sphere he can and must join the writer in his search for an "original text." And if the writer, in his turn, admits the "original text" of revelation into his search for the "original text" of this world, if he remains—or becomes—open to the Biblical word, then the writer and the Christian can meet. Then each has existence, reality, meaning, language, even criticism to impart to the other.

Here, too, is a problem. For the writer, language means the presentation of what is visual, audible, of the sensual event. For the Christian, there has existed from the beginning the problem that the object of his belief is not seeable, can never be adequately presented in human language. There were times when the Christian so overplayed this aspect that it was transformed into an extraordinary and almost naïve figurativeness. There were times when theologians and preachers, with a matter-of-courseness that is hard to understand, spoke very categorically (in worldly and philosophical categories) about their God-Object. Since there has been a dialectical theology, people have become more sharply aware of the insufficiency of categorical speech, of the incomparable, the incomprehensible, the invisible, of a God Who is beyond human experience. Mockers and unbelievers who insist on a reality that can be exhibited, on some mode of identifying God and His activity, as though it were all happening in a film, have taken the easy way. The tendency to let only this kind of film reality count for real is not new among artists and writers today. They know, of course, about the reality of the psychic, about those experiences of man's consciousness that can hardly be objectified. But they reject as a basic deception the possibility that God may enter the psyche, that a change in consciousness may bear the stamp of "supernatural" faith. A part of science has preceded them along this road.

I cannot escape the impression that many writers are not so unprejudiced, so generous, so up-to-date, so up-to-yesterday as many radio studios pretend, as many feuilletons would have us believe. Often one has the impression that the question of language is also a question of power for the writers. "Men of letters have taken over the role of the clergy," wrote Saul Bellow. He quoted Walt Whitman: "The priests depart, the divine literatus arrives."[18]

Belief and literature, the role of the Christian and a literature that struggles to express existence, should, it seems to me, be concerned with taking down fences, with a reacceptance of the man who has achieved success, with powerlessness amid the powerful institutions of this world, with suffering this world—and themselves, perhaps with poverty. What did Gottfried Benn say? "Let us talk together / He who does not speak is dead."[19]

# Notes

## *Chapter 1*

[1]For the translation of this poem, I am indebted to Sister Thérèse Sullivan, Professor Emeritus of English, Trinity College, Washington, D.C. [Translator's note.] The German text reads as follows:

> *Der Mensch*
> Mensch! O hoher Name, Himmelswonne
> Giesst allmächtig sich dem Herzen ein
> Aus dem Lichtmeer jener Geistersonne,
> Denk' ich, o Erschaffner, dein.
> Herrlich gingst du aus des Schöpfers Händen:
> Dich unsterblich selber zu vollenden
> Gab der Meister dir die hohe Kraft,
> Gab dir Mut, das Schwerste zu erleiden,
> Wenn sich Rflicht und Neigung feindlich scheiden
> Auf dem Meer der Leidenschaft.
>
> Mensch! O hehres Meisterstück des Himmels,
> . . . . . . . . . . . . . . . . . . . . . . . . . . . . . . . . . . . . . . . .

[2]*Menschheitsdämmerung. Ein Dokument des Expressionismus*, ed. Kurt Pinthus (Hamburg, 1920; latest edition: Rowohlt Klassiker, nos. 55–56: Hamburg, 1959), pp. 25, 27. Cf. Georg Kaiser's drama, *Die Bürger von Calais:* "Tonight, I have seen the new man."

[3]Ibid., p. 28 f.

[4]*Literatur und Dichtung im Dritten Reich*, ed. Josef Wulf (Hamburg, 1966), p. 51.

[5]Bergengruen's *Dies Irae* was published in 1945 by Desch in Munich. The volume

was reprinted in 1948 by the Haus und Schule Publishing Company in West Berlin (sixth to tenth thousand). Hagelstange's *Venezianisches Credo* was first published in 1945 (155 copies printed by hand in Verona). The poems became widely known only after they had been reprinted by the Insel Publishing Company (Wiesbaden, 1946).

[6]The German text reads as follows:

Völker der Welt, der Ruf des Gerichts gilt uns allen.
Alle verklagt das gemeinsam Verrat'ne, gemeinsam Entweihte.
Völker, vernehmt mit uns allen das göttliche: Metanoeite!

[7]For the translation of this poem, I am indebted to Sister Thérèse Sullivan, Professor Emeritus of English, Trinity College, Washington, D.C. [Translator's note.] The German text reads as follows:

Was heisst denn das: ein Mensch? Ist Gang und Rede
genug, um sich als Herr der Welt zu meinen,
als Ebenbild des Ahnen und des Einen,
der uns berufen hat und dem jedwede

der Kreaturen lebt, ihm Lob zu sagen?
Was wiegt der Dank, den unser Mund beteuert?
Der Atem gilt, der unsere Brust befeuert,
das Opfer, das wir ohne Arglist wagen.

Denn uns beschämt der Vogel und die Blume,
der Käfer und der Fisch, ja selbst der tote
und kalte Stein im Bach, der dem Gebote

der Strömung still gehorcht, wenn wir nicht wissen,
Licht zu gewinnen aus den Finsternissen
und Mehrer sein an unserm Menschentume.

From *Venezianisches Credo* (Wiesbaden, 1946), p. 32.

[8]The German text reads as follows:

Begraben vom Emaillehimmel
Des raschen Sterbens lebt ihr nun
Und schüttet aus der Wasserflasche
Euch Heiterkeit auf euer Ruhn.

Das Leid zerschmilzt euch sanft im Nacken.
Die Silbenrätsel sind gelöst
Der Worte, ihre tiefen Schatten:
Angst, die die Nacht euch eingeflösst.

Erinn'rung, wie ein Ei zerflossen,
Quält euch nicht mehr, die ihr mich grüsst.
Ihr habt die Läufe der Gewehre
Vergessen schon, die ihr durchsüsst.

Von Träumen, eurem Ebenbilde
Und einem andern Leben seid.
Ihr braucht die Hände aus den Taschen
Nicht mehr zu ziehen, schlagbereit.

[9]The German text reads as follows:

*Inventur*
Dies ist meine Mütze,
dies ist mein Mantel,
hier ist mein Rasierzeug
im Beutel aus Leinen.

Konservenbüchse:
Mein Teller, mein Becher,
ich hab in das Weissblech
den Namen geritzt.

Geritzt hier mit diesem
kostbaren Nagel,
den vor begehrlichen
Augen ich berge.

Im Brotbeutel sind
ein Paar wollene Socken
und einiges, was ich
niemand verrate,

so dient es als Kissen
nachts meinem Kopf.
Die Pappe hier liegt
zwischen mir und der Erde.

Die Bleistiftmine
lieb ich am meisten:
Tags schreibt sie mir Verse,
die nachts ich erdacht.

Dies ist mein Notizbuch,
dies meine Zeltbahn,
dies ist mein Handtuch,
dies ist mein Zwirn.

[10]The German text reads as follows:

*Rückkehr*
Die Vaterstadt, wie find ich sie doch?
folgend den Bomberschwärmen
Komm ich nach Haus.

## Chapter 1

Wo denn liegt sie? Wo die ungeheuren
Gebirge von Rauch stehen.
Das in den Feuern dort
Ist sie.

Die Vaterstadt, wie empfängt sie mich wohl?
Vor mir kommen die Bomber. Tödliche Schwärme
Melden euch meine Rückkehr. Feuersbrünste
Gehen dem Sohn voraus.

[11]Wilhelm Grenzmann, *Deutsche Dichtung der Gegenwart*, 2nd edition (Frankfurt, 1955), chapter title and pp. 398 ff.

[12]See the present volume, pp. 74–94, for an account of the origin and development of "Group 47."

[13]Walter Jens, *Deutsche Literatur der Gegenwart* (Munich, 1961; Deutscher Taschenbuch Verlag: Munich, 1964), p. 130.

[14]Revised version in *Einzelheiten* (Frankfurt, 1962), pp. 255–272.

[15]Since publishing the poems in *Die gestundete Zeit and Anrufung des Grossen Bären* and a third volume of collected works under the title *Gedichte, Erzählungen, Hörspiel, Essays* (Munich, 1964), Ingeborg Bachmann has fallen silent. Four poems in *Kursbuch 15* (1968) reveal a deep sense of injury and the withdrawal of the lyric *I* from this hopelessly divided world that had already been apparent in the poem "Exile" in the volume of collected works. "Böhmen liegt am Meer" is the title of the last poem in *Kursbuch 15*. The last two strophes read:

I border still on a word and on another land,
I border, yet how little, more and more on all,
a Bohemian, wanderer, owning nothing, held by nothing,
my only boon—to behold my chosen land from a contested sea.

[16]See the present volume, pp. 39–64, for a further discussion of Günter Grass's lyric.

[17]Beat generation (literally, the generation that feels itself beaten, exhausted; cf. Immermann's concept of "epigones" in 1830–1836) is a collective designation for a part of the second post-war generation in North America, the angry young men who conduct themselves with extreme nonconformism, aggression, and self-complacency toward government and civilization in the contemporary world. Walter Höllerer and Gregory Corso have presented this beat generation in a dual-language anthology *Junge Amerikanische Lyrik* (Munich, 1961).

[18]Bertolt Brecht, *Gesammelte Werke. Werkausgabe* (Frankfurt, 1967), Vol. 8, pp. 267 ff.; Vol. 9, p. 818. Enzensberger's *verteidigung der wölfe* (1957) is hereafter cited as V; *landessprache* (1960) is hereafter cited as L.

[19]"viertel" [here translated "quarters"] = "Stadtviertel" ["section of the city"]; "the deadly powder finely ground": cf. Günter Eich's poem, published in 1951: "Wake up, for your dreams are bad," especially the last line, which reads: "Be uncomfortable, be sand, not oil in the machinery of the world!" It would require a separate work to show how strikingly the number of admonitory poems increased in the 50s. The German text of *ins lesebuch für die oberstufe* reads as follows:

## Chapter 1

*ins lesebuch für die oberstufe*

lies keine oden, mein sohn, lies die fahrpläne:
sie sind genauer.roll die seekarten auf,
eh es zu spät ist.sei wachsam, sing nicht.
der tag kommt, wo sie wieder listen ans tor
schlagen und malen den neinsagern auf die brust
zinken.lern unerkannt gehn,lern mehr als ich:
das viertel wechseln, den pass, das gesicht.
versteh dich auf den kleinen verrat,
die tägliche schmutzige rettung.nützlich
sind die enzykliken zum feueranzünden,
die manifeste: butter einzuwickeln und salz
für die wehrlosen, wut und geduld sind nötig,
in die lungen der macht zu blasen
den feinen tödlichen staub, gemahlen
von denen,die viel gelernt haben,
die genau sind,von dir (V 85).

[20]The German text reads as follows:

*verteidigung der wölfe gegen die lämmer*

soll der geier vergissmeinnicht fressen?
was verlangt ihr vom schakal,
dass er sich häute, vom wolf? soll
er sich selber ziehen die zähne?
was gefällt euch nicht
an politruks und an päpsten,
was guckt ihr blöd aus der wäsche
auf den verlogenen bildschirm?
wer näht denn dem general
den blutstreif an seine hose? wer
zerlegt vor dem wucherer den kapaun?
wer hängt sich stolz das blechkreuz
vor den knurrenden nabel? wer
nimmt das trinkgeld, den silberling,
den schweigepfennig? es gibt
viel bestohlene, wenig diebe; wer
applaudiert ihnen denn, wer
steckt die abzeichen an, wer
lechzt nach der lüge?

seht in den spiegel: feig,
scheuend die mühsal der wahrheit,
dem lernen abgeneigt, das denken
überantwortend den wölfen,
der nasenring euer teuerster schmuck,
keine täuschung zu dumm, kein trost

zu billig, jede erpressung
ist für euch noch zu milde.

ihr lämmer, schwestern sind,
mit euch verglichen, die krähen:
ihr blendet einer den andern.
brüderlichkeit herrscht
unter den wölfen:
sie gehn in rudeln.

gelobt sein die räuber: ihr,
einladend zur vergewaltigung,
werft euch aufs faule bett
des gehorsams, winselnd noch
lügt ihr. zerrissen
wollt ihr werden, ihr
ändert die welt nicht (V 90 f.).

[21]Cf Gottfried Benn, *Können Dichter die Welt ändern?* (1930); *Über die Rolle des Schriftstellers in dieser Zeit* (1929); *Soll die Dichtung das Leben bessern?* (1955) in *Gesammelte Werke* (Wiesbaden, 1959–1961), Vol. IV, pp. 213 ff., 205 ff.; Vol. I, pp. 583 ff.

[22]Benn wanted to "captivate things mystically by the word" *(Gesammelte Werke*, Vol. III, p. 196). Brecht wrote in 1927: "Without doubt, lyric must be something that people will be able to judge on its utilitarian value" *(Schriften zur Literatur und Kunst*, Vol. I [Frankfurt, 1969], p. 69). Enzensberger says: The poem is "a technical production in the Greek sense and, at the same time, a utilitarian object" (in *Mein Gedicht ist mein Messer. Lyriker zu ihren Gedichten*, ed. Hans Bender [Erw. Taschenbuchausgabe: Munich, List 1961], p. 144.

[23]The German text reads as follows:

*landessprache*

. . . . . . . . . . .
hier geht es aufwärts,
hier ist gut sein,
wo es rückwärts aufwärts geht,
hier schiesst der leitende herr den leitenden herrn
mit dem gesangbuch ab,
hier führen die leichtbeschädigten mit den
schwerbeschädigten krieg,
hier heisst es unerbittlich nett zueinander sein,
. . . . . . . . . . . . . . . . . . . . . . . . . . . . . . . . . . . . . . .
hier lasst uns hütten bauen,
auf diesem arischen schrotthaufen,
auf diesem krächzenden parkplatz,
wo aus den ruinen ruinen sprossen,
nagelneu, ruinen auf vorrat, auf raten,
auf abruf, auf widerruf:

hiersein ist herrlich,
. . . . . . . . . . . . . . . . .

in dieser mördergrube,
wo der kalendar sich selber abreisst vor ohnmacht und hast,
wo die vergangenheit in den müllschluckern schwelt
und die zukunft mit falschen zähnen knirscht,
das kommt davon, dass es aufwärts geht,
da tun wir fleckenwasser drauf,
das ist hier so üblich, das wundert mich nicht,
goldrichtig liegen wir hier,
wo das positive zum höchstkurs notiert,
die handelskammern decken sich damit ein
und bahren es auf unter panzerglas,

wo wir uns finden wohl unter blinden,
in den schau–, kauf–, und zeughäusern,
. . . . . . . . . . . . . . . . . . . . . . . . . . . . . . .
was habe ich hier verloren, was suche ich
und stochre in diesem unzuständigen knäuel
von nahkampfspangen, genussscheinen,
gamsbärten, schlussverkäufen, und finde nichts
als chronische, chronologische turnhallen
und sachbearbeiter für die menschlichkeit
in den kasernen für die kasernen für die kasernen:
was soll ich hier? und was soll ich sagen
in welcher sprache? und wem?
. . . . . . . . . . . . . . . . . . . . . . . . . .
deutschland, mein land, unheilig herz der völker,
ziemlich verrufen, von fall zu fall
. . . . . . . . . . . . . . . . . . . . . .(L 7–13).

[24]The German text reads as follows:

mein land, ich verschone dich nicht,
ich halte dich, selber sterblich,
in dieses sterbliche licht (L 75).

[25]The German text reads as follows:

Da fiel uns Ikarus vor die Füsse,
schrie: Treibt Gattung, Kinder!
Rein ins schlechtgelüftete Thermopylä! -
Warf uns einen seiner Unterschenkel hinterher,
schlug um, war alle.

[26]*Gesammelte Werke*, Vol. III, pp. 26, 46f.

[27]The German text reads as follows:

Mensch, Völkerschlachten, Katalaunen
hinab den Bestienschlund.

Chapter 1

> Die Welt zerdacht. Und Raum und Zeiten
> und was die Menschheit wob und wog.
> Funktion nur von Unendlichkeiten -
> die Mythe log.

[28]*Irdisches Vergnügen in g* (Hamburg, 1959), p. 37; hereafter abbreviated as I. Between 1721 and 1748, the Hamburg senator, Barthold Heinrich Brockes, published the poem *Irdisches Vergnügen in Gott* in eight parts. Brockes was a son of the Enlightenment. He wanted his poem to give religious edification and to further belief in God and a happy religious life. He was strongly influenced by the *Demonstration de l'existence de Dieu* of Archbishop Fénelon of Cambrai (Paris, 1713). Fénelon proved the existence, truth, and goodness of God from the beauty and purposefulness of nature and its usefulness to man. Rühmkorf's small "g" is, in the first place, an ironical and satirical transposition of the word "Gott," which was originally written with a capital letter. But the small "g" is also the symbol used in physics for the acceleration of gravity in earthly bodies. Rühmkorf speaks frequently of falling and of earth. He obviously intends to draw an ironic relationship between God and physics, between Anti-Icarus and the acceleration of gravity, between mystical hope and the demythologized experience of bodies.

[29]I 29. Heinrich Heine had already said: "The heavens we abandon / To angels and sparrows." That already represents a formal destruction of the sublime by juxtaposition with the not sublime: angels and sparrows (in *Deutschland. Ein Wintermärchen*, I, 1844). The ailing Heine of the avowals confessed then: "The time of vanity is past." "I returned to the lowly fold of God's creatures, and I pay homage to the omnipotence of a highest being. . . . Since then, the existence of God has been more than just a source of salvation for me. . . ." (*Gesammelte Werke*, ed. E. Elster [Leipzig and Vienna, n.d.], Vol. VI, pp. 66, 49 f.). The German poem reads as follows:

> Die Schotten auf, Bewusstseinsboom,
> —janz schpätes Haus—
> und hebst den Kopf voll Alterthum
> und schlappst die Himmelsschüssel aus.
> . . . . . . . . . . . . . . . . . . . . . . . . . . . . . . . . .
> Du nicht, du bist nicht auserwählt,
> da trittst du leer und glaubtest schon
> die Schuppen auf dem Kopf gezählt,
> mein Sohn, verlorener Sohn.
> . . . . . . . . . . . . . . . . . . . . . . . .
> Figuren in den Sand geschifft,
> Lenin und Winnetou . . .
>
> Historischen Moments,
> ach, welchen Tages Ausgeburt –?–
> Du bleibst, der seine Brocken schnorrt
> im Mulm der Existenz.

[30]Benn, *Gesammelte Werke*, Vol. III, p. 216 ("Oh, when all tended toward one center"); Vol. III, p. 157.

[31]The German poem reads as follows:

Prächtig, nichts verstanden zu haben und doch
sein Nasenloch voll Sterblichkeit zu geniessen–:
der wackere Sohn des Moments,
jetzo schlendernd unter viel Feinden und wenig Brüdern,
durch Schaden schlau geworden und
dem Boden gründlich misstrauend, von dem er sich
  geschaffen wähnt . . .

trottet er, bar jeden höheren Zieles,
kantapper—kantapper,
ein asthenischer Wolf ins Orangenlicht,
. . . . . . . . . . . . . . . . . . . . . . . . . . . . . . . . .

sein Fell sich glättend, seine verstauchten Strukturen,
wenn aus sirupner Umarmung er sich nachdenklich löst—
. . . . . . . . . . . . . . . . . . . . . . . . . . . . . . . . . . . . . . . . . . . . . .

Das Hohelied des Ungehorsams—
gebellt oder verkündet–
aber von keinem bisher so prägnant
als von ihm (I 23).

[32] Rühmkorf, *Kunststücke. Fünfzig Gedichte nebst einer Anleitung zum Widerspruch* (Hamburg, 1962), p. 48.

[33]The German poems read as follows:

Es gibt uns noch, Kameraden, unwiderlegbar,
—und bewiese uns nur das Fleisch, das sich warm in der Hose bewegt—
lauter stammelt der Sterbliche:
Coeo ergo sum! (I 32).
. . . . . . . . . . . . . . . . .

Ich vom Boden, jawohl, von der Erde, ich, von den Steinen,
keine Kondore mehr im hirnenen Horst–!
Wer ist gekommen, Aufschwung und Fall zu beweinen
des geflügelten Aff, wenn er Furcht in den Äther morst?
(I 37).

[34]Rühmkorf, *Kunststücke*, p. 134.

[35]The German poem reads as follows:

Der zu leben sich einschliesst
Muss wissen
Warum er gestern zur Nachtzeit erwachte
Wohin er heute durch die Strassen geht
Wozu er morgen in seinem Zimmer
Die Wände mit weissem Kalk anstreicht.

War da ein Schrei?
Ist da ein Ziel?
Wird da Sicherheit sein?

[36]Günter Kunert, *Verkündigung des Wetters* (Munich, 1966), p. 48.
[37]Ibid., pp. 49 f. The German poem reads as follows:

*Ikarus* 64
1
Fliegen ist schwer:
Jede Hand klebt am Gehebel von Maschinen:
Geldesbedürftig.
Geheftet die Füsse
An Gaspedal und Tanzparkett. Fest eingenietet
Der Kopf im stolzen im fortschrittlichen
im vorurteilsharten
Sturzhelm.
2
Ballast: Das mundwarme Eisbein
In der Familiengruft des Magens.
Ballast: Das finstere Blut
Gestaut an hervorragender Stelle
Gürtelwärts.
Töne
Erster zweiter neunter dreissigster Symphonien
Ohrhoch gestapelt zu kulturellem Übergewicht.
Verpulverte Vergangenheit
In handlichen Urnen verpackt.
Tankweise Tränen im Vorrat unabwerfbare:
Fliegen ist schwer.
3
Dennoch breite die Arme aus und nimm
Einen Anlauf für das Unmögliche.
Nimm einen langen Anlauf damit du
Hinfliegst
Zu deinem Himmel
Daran alle Sterne verlöschen.
4
Denn Tag wird.
Ein Horizont zeigt sich immer.
Nimm einen Anlauf.

[38]*Fahrt ins Staublose* (Frankfurt, 1961), pp. 92–94. The German text reads as follows:

Wenn die Propheten einbrächen
durch Türen der Nacht
mit ihren Worten Wunden reissend
in die Felder der Gewohnheit,

ein weit Entlegenes hereinholend
für den Tagelöhner
der längst nicht mehr wartet am Abend–

Wenn die Propheten einbrächen
durch Türen der Nacht
und ein Ohr wie eine Heimat suchten–

Ohr der Menschheit
du nesselverwachsenes,
würdest du hören?
. . . . . . . . . . . . . .
Wenn die Propheten aufständen
in der Nacht der Menschheit
wie Liebende, die das Herz des Geliebten suchen,
Nacht der Menschheit
hättest du ein Herz zu vergeben?

In the Frankfurt (1961) edition of the poems, the last line reads: "würdest du ein Herz zu vergessen haben?" [would you have a heart to forget?].

[39]Among the more recent political poems in song and chanson are: *Kürbiskern-Songbuch*, ed. Manfred Vosz (Munich, 1968); *Chanson 67*, ed. Helmut König (Bad Godesberg, 1968); Volker von Törne, *Wolfspelz. Gedichte / Lieder / Montagen* (Berlin, 1968); Wolf Biermann, *Mit Marx- und Engelszungen* (Berlin, 1968).

[40]On the subject of this distrust, see Günter Herburger, "Dogmatisches über Gedichte," in *Kursbuch 10* (1967), pp. 150–161. Herburger himself wants to write "poems like overstuffed drawers that stick" (p. 160), an extreme montage structured to describe in sweeping arcs or to tell a story—or to describe *and* tell a story—that does not exclude the lyric *I*. Günter Grass has expressed his criticism *(Ausgefragt* [Neuwied and Berlin, 1967], pp. 75 f.) of the political poem of protest as "industrial trend" and interstice ("The costs of production are small. / Take one-eighth of just wrath, / two-eights of daily annoyance / and, to give it foretaste, five-eights of powerless rage.").

[41]Biermann in East Berlin and Grass in West Berlin are writing for a better democracy; of late, Enzensberger and the writers of the "kürbiskern" have been writing for a revolution *(Vierteljahrschrift für Literatur und Kritik*, published since 1965 in Munich).

## *Chapter 2*

[1]The plays *Hochwasser* (1955; new version, 1963), *Onkel, Onkel* (1955–1957; new version, 1965); *Die bösen Köche* (written 1957, publ. 1961) are not so well known.

[2]The German text, which is printed on the flap of the volume, reads as follows:

*Die Vorzüge der Windhühner*
Weil sie kaum Platz einnehmen
auf ihrer Stange aus Zugluft
und nicht nach meinen zahmen Stühlen picken.

Weil sie die harten Traumrinden nicht verschmähen,
nicht den Buchstaben nachlaufen,
die der Briefträger jeden Morgen vor meiner Tür verliert.
Weil sie stehen bleiben,
von der Brust bis zur Fahne
eine duldsame Fläche, ganz klein beschrieben,
keine Feder vergessen, kein Apostroph . . .
Weil sie die Tür offen lassen,
der Schlüssel die Allegorie bleibt,
die dann und wann kräht.
Weil ihre Eier so leicht sind
und bekömmlich, durchsichtig.
Wer sah diesen Augenblick schon,
da das Gelb genug hat, die Ohren anlegt und verstummt.
Weil diese Stille so weich ist,
das Fleisch am Kinn einer Venus
nähre ich sie.—
Oft bei Ostwind,
wenn die Zwischenwände umblättern,
ein neues Kapitel sich auftut,
lehne ich glücklich am Zaun,
ohne die Hühner zählen zu müssen,—
weil sie zahllos sind und sich ständig vermehren.

[3]*Die Vorzüge der Windhühner* (Berlin and Neuwied, 1956), pp. 39–42. "Fünf Vögel" is the only prose work in the volume. It resembles a fable in verse. The closeness of prose to poetry and of poetry to prose is a frequent phenomenon in the works of contemporary authors. See, for instance, the works of Brecht or Heissenbüttel. On the motif of birds, cf. the scarecrow ballet in the novel *Hundejahre* (pp. 400 ff.) and the poem "Vogelscheuchen" (in *Gleisdreieck*, pp. 34–35). The poem is not so forceful as the prose work and probably belongs to an earlier date.

[4]See Hans Arp, *Wortträume und schwarze Sterne. Auswahl aus den Gedichten 1911–1952* (Wiesbaden, 1953).

[5]*Gleisdreieck*, p. 11. The volumes of poems are hereafter abbreviated as follows: *Die Vorzüge der Windhühner*=W, *Gleisdreieck*=G, *Ausgefragt*=A. "Gleisdreieck" is a station on the elevated railway near the sector boundary between East and West Berlin. On the metaphor of the spider, cf. the poem "Die Dämonen der Stadt" by the young poet Georg Heym, who was drowned in the Havel River in Berlin in 1912.

[6]"Dreiecke . . . Hühner": cf. W 18; "In the right ear, Gleisdreieck, / an Advent hymn in the left ear" (W 48).

[7]The German text reads as follows:

Ich grüsse Berlin, indem ich
dreimal meine Stirn an eine
der Brandmauern schlage.

[8]The German text reads as follows:

Gnade Gnade.
Die grosse Trümmerfrau
hat einen Plan entworfen,
dem jeder Stein unterliegen wird.
Der grosse Ziegelbrenner will mitmachen.

[9]"Sechsundsechzig" (1966 in Berlin), A 93.
[10]The German text reads as follows.

*Im Ei*
Wir leben im Ei.
Die Innenseite der Schale
haben wir mit unanständigen Zeichnungen
und den Vornamen unserer Feinde bekritzelt.
Wir werden gebrütet.

Wer uns auch brütet,
unseren Bleistift brütet er mit.
Ausgeschlüpft eines Tages,
werden wir uns sofort
ein Bildnis des Brütenden machen.

Wir nehmen an, dass wir gebrütet werden.
Wir stellen uns ein gutmütiges Geflügel vor
und schreiben Schulaufsätze
über Farbe und Rasse
der uns brütenden Henne.

Wann schlüpfen wir aus?
Unsere Propheten im Ei
streiten sich für mittelmässige Bezahlung
über die Dauer der Brutzeit.
Sie nehmen einen Tag X an.

Aus Langeweile und echtem Bedürfnis
haben wir Brutkästen erfunden.
Wir sorgen uns sehr um unseren Nachwuchs im Ei.
Gerne würden wir jener, die über uns wacht
unser Patent empfehlen.

Wir aber haben ein Dach überm Kopf.
Senile Küken,
Embryos mit Sprachkenntnissen
reden den ganzen Tag
und besprechen noch ihre Träume.

Und wenn wir nun nicht gebrütet werden?
Wenn diese Schale niemals ein Loch bekommt?
Wenn unser Horizont nur der Horizont

unserer Kritzeleien ist und auch bleiben wird?
Wir hoffen, dass wir gebrütet werden.

Wenn wir auch nur noch vom Brüten reden,
bleibt doch zu befürchten, dass jemand,
ausserhalb unserer Schale, Hunger verspürt,
uns in die Pfanne haut und mit Salz bestreut.—
Was machen wir dann, ihr Brüder im Ei?

[11]In the last strophe, it becomes obvious that the egg is not a pictorial symbol, but a reflective one, that it has been developed as an allegorical image. The pictorial symbol would not permit the man who feels hunger to "break... into a pan" an egg that is ready to be hatched, since he would know that it would be unpalatable. On the motif of the hen, see also G 23–24, 67, 71, 77.

Günter Grass's poem "Im Ei" has found imitators among the Primaner poets. The poem "gesang im ei" by Rainer Wulf (b. July 13, 1945 in Hamburg) tells how this poet sees himself and his friends, his enemies and his own hatched hero-figure in the egg ("i am argus i am hercules i / am orestes i am ulysses")—quadruply powerful, alert, wise, and strong *(Primanerlyrik* [rororo Nr. 795: Hamburg, 1965], p. 8 f.).

[12]The German text reads as follows:

fromm, eine Zigarette,
senkrecht glaubt sie,
senkrecht die Spinne ein Lot,
geht jeder Untief nach–

[13]The German text reads as follows:

Man sagt:
Er will den Hähnen die Zukunft nehmen.
Er geht den Hühnern nach,
als gehe es darum, das Ei zu verbessern.

Man sagt:
Er glaubt an Geflügel.
Der Heilige Geist grüsst ihn
in Gestalt einer Henne.

Das alles ist üble Nachrede,
und Wahrheit schreibt so:
Manchmal quält mich der Zahnschmerz,
dann geht es mir wieder besser;

besonders an Sonntagen
wird mir gewiss,
dass solch ein Hinweis
auch Freude bereiten kann.

Später erst,
wenn dieses Gebiss
nicht mehr den einen Nerv betont,
kaue ich Kummer

und sehe den Amseln zu,
—es müssen nicht Hühner
und Hähne sein—
bis dass mir schwarz wird vor Augen.

[14]*Ausgefragt. Gedichte und Zeichnungen* (Luchterhand: Neuwied, 1967); "Der Delphin," A 47.

[15]The German poem reads as follows:

Ich, gelehrig, sah im Sprung meinen Lehrer:
den Konvertiten hinter dem Mikrophon.
Hörte ihn abschwören und zerlachte ihm seine Beichte.
Schülergelächter. Delphinengelächter.
Er stülpte sich um, lächerlich um:
Damals war ich, heute bin ich.
Doch als er altbackenen Kuchen erbrochen
und frische Semmel getischt hatte,
als Saulus, gleich nach der Häutung,
in mir,—ich sprang!—
den belehrbaren Delphin entdeckte,
als ich dran glauben sollte, dran glauben sollte,
säuerte Angst mein Gelächter:
ich sicherte den Ausgang,
tauchte und schwamm mich frei.

[16]Alfred Döblin, *Aufsätze zur Literatur* (Olten and Freiburg, 1963), pp. 396, 398.

[17]The German poem reads as follows:

Wie sieht es aus?—Es sah schon schlimmer aus.
Du hattest Glück?—Es lag am Köder.
Und was hast du gemacht seitdem?
In Büchern steht, wie es sich besser machte.
Ich meine, was hast du getan?
Ich war dagegen. Immer schon dagegen.
Und wurdest schuldig?—Nein. Ich tat ja nichts.
Und hast erkannt, was sich erkennen liess?
Ja. Ich erkannte Gummi mit der Faust.
Und deine Hoffnung?—Log die Wüste grün.
Und deine Wut?—Sie klirrt als Eis im Glas.
Die Scham?—Wir grüssen uns von fern.
Dein grosser Plan?—Zahlt sich zur Hälfte aus.
Hast du vergessen?—Neuerdings, mein Kopf.
Und die Natur?—Oft fahr ich dran vorbei.
Die Menschen?—Seh ich gern im Film.
Sie sterben wieder.—Ja. Ich las davon . . .

## Chapter 2

[18]The German poem reads as follows:

> Als sie mich traf,
> traf ihr Gegenstand meine Seele,
> die ihr wie ein Gegenstand ist.

[19]The German poem reads as follows:

> Immer lehnte ich ab,
> von einer schattenlosen Idee
> meinen schattenwerfenden Körper
> verletzen zu lassen.

[20]The German poem reads as follows:

> *Politische Landschaft*
> Uns Geschädigten, denen das Wissen
> Mühe macht beim Verlernen,
> ordnet die Geografie wirre Geschichte:
> Seitlich Adenau und bis an das Flüsschen Hunte,
> zwischen Galen und Frings,
> buchen die Sozis kleine Gewinne,
> mühen sich ab beim Verlernen.
>
> wo immer sich ernste Berge im Wege stehn
> und der Gedanke nicht flügge wird,
> lohnen sich Blicke
> vom Blessing über den Rhein.
> O, ihr linken und rechten Nebenflüsse:
> die Barzel fliesst in die Wehner.
> Abwässer speisen das Sein
> Grauwacke, Rehwinkel, laubgesägt Tannen,
> Karst, Abs und Kulmbacher Bier,
> altfränkische Wolken über dem Heideggerland.

It is impossible to convey the political innuendoes of the poem in translation. The following remarks may prove helpful. *Adenau,* a small city in the Eifel region; the allusion is to Konrad Adenauer (1876–1967), former chancellor of the Federal Republic of Germany. *Hunte,* a tributary of the Weser River; the allusion is to Alois Hundhammer (b. 1900), leading member of the Christian Socialist Party of Bavaria. *Galen,* Clemens August Graf von (1878–1946), Cardinal of Münster, strong opponent of the Nazis. *Frings,* Joseph (b. 1887), Cardinal of Cologne, official leader of German Catholics. *Sozis* (a word formed on the analogy of *Nazis):* the Social Democrats. *Blessing,* Karl (b. 1900), German banker and industrialist; since 1958, President of the Deutsche Bundesbank. *Barzel,* Rainer (b. 1924), German politician; member of the Christian Democratic Party. *Wehner,* Herbert (b. 1906), German politician; formerly a Communist, but now a member of the Social Democratic Party. *Sein:* in Heidegger's philosophy, *sein* = "being." By association with the words *Grauwacke* and *Karst* in succeeding lines, however, *Sein* may refer to the Seine River, which rises in limestone areas and is linked to the Rhine River by canal. *Grauwacke* (Eng.:

graywacke), a limestone-like sediment (cf. *A Glossary of Geographical Terms*, ed. Sir Dudley Stamp, 2nd edition [London, 1966], p. 221). *Rehwinkel*, Edmund (b. 1899), German politician; President of the Deutscher Bauernverband. *Tannen:* fir trees. *Karst* (from: Karst region of Adriatic): "areas of 'solution fretwork' " (cf. *A Glossary of Geographical Terms*, pp. 277–278). *Abs*, Hermann Josef (b. 1901), German banker; led German delegation in 1952 at London Conference on German External Debts. *Kulmbach*, city in Upper Franconia; noted, among other things, for its brewery. *Heidegger-land* = Baden (in SW Germany). [Translator's note.]

[21]Günter Grass, *Über meinen Lehrer Döblin und andere Vorträge* (Berlin, 1968), p. 63.

## *Chapter 3*

[1]*Wozu Lyrik heute. Dichtung und Leser in einer gesteuerten Gesellschaft* (Munich, 1968).

[2]Emil Staiger, *Grundbegriffe der Poetik* (Atlantis Publishing Co.: Zurich, 1946). Hugo Friedrich, *Die Struktur der modernen Lyrik* in *Rowohlts deutsche Enzyklopädie* (Reinbek, 1956). Staiger defended and refined his concept of "lyric and lyrical" in *Deutschunterricht*, Heft 2 (1952). This article was reprinted by Reinhold Grimm, *Zur Lyrik-Diskussion* (Darmstadt, 1966). Also to be found here is the formula, which has since become famous, that defines interpretation as "grasping what grips us" ("begreifen, was uns ergreift").

[3]*Zur Lyrik-Diskussion* (Darmstadt, 1966).

[4]*Immanente Ästhetik. Ästhetische Reflexion. Lyrik als Paradigma der Moderne*, ed. W. Iser (Munich, 1966). Clemens Heselhaus had already revealed himself as one of the best contemporary German experts on the lyric in his book *Deutsche Lyrik der Moderne von Nietzsche bis Yvan Goll* (Düsseldorf, 1962).

[5]*Ein Gedicht und sein Autor. Lyrik und Essay*, ed. and with an introduction by Walter Höllerer (Berlin, 1967, *Literarisches Colloquium)*. In December 1965, Höllerer published *Theorie der modernen Lyrik. Dokumente zur Poetik I* (rde 231–233). Sixty poets, from Coleridge to Różewicz (nearly the whole of the European and a good part of the American tradition), express significant views on poetry.

[6]It is a pity that Domin, in her consideration of literary norms, did not extend her remarks to the works of Max Wehrli *(Wert und Unwert in der Dichtung* [Cologne, 1965] and Walter Müller-Seidel *(Probleme der literarischen Wertung* [Stuttgart, 1965]). A glance at Höllerer's *Dokumente zur Poetik I* and, more especially, at his volume *Lyrik und Essay* would have been very interesting. The poem on the level of criticism (in contrast to the poem on the level of poetry), that is, the problem of the poem as criticism of society, could also have been treated more intensively by Domin. The linguistic and textual attempts of Gomringer and Heissenbüttel and of the Viennese school were unfortunately not considered.

## *Chapter 4*

[1]Christian Mayer-Amery and Wolfgang Hildesheimer in *Gruppe 47. Die Polemik um die deutsche Gegenwartsliteratur. Eine Dokumentation*, ed. H. Ziermann (wolter editionen: Frankfurt, 1966), pp. 62, 110. Since this volume reproduces the reports and discussions in conjunction with the meeting at Princeton, it will hereafter be

cited as P. Günter Blöcker's reproaches in *Die Zeit* (1962) have been reprinted in *Die Gruppe 47. Bericht, Kritik, Polemik. Ein Handbuch*, ed. R. Lettau (Luchterhand: Neuwied and Berlin, 1967), pp. 353 ff. This work is hereafter cited as H. It appeared for the twentieth anniversary of the founding of the Group. It was preceded by the *Almanach der Gruppe 47*, which appeared for the fifteenth anniversary. It was edited by H. W. Richter (Rowohlt: Hamburg, 1962) and is hereafter cited as A. The polemics of Neumann and Nossack are to be found (in an abbreviated form) in P 77 ff., 92 ff. The first opponent of the Group was Friedrich Sieburg, who published his remarks in 1952 in *Die Zeit*. The later literary critics of *Die Zeit*—R. W. Leonhard, M. Reich-Ranicki, D. E. Zimmer—were present as critics at the meetings of the Group. Reich-Ranicki belonged to the five best critics of the Group.

[2]Golo Mann, *Deutsche Geshichte des 19 und 20. Jahrhunderts* (Frankfurt, 1966), p. 985.

[3]H. W. Richter in *Almanach der Gruppe 47*, p. 11, and in *Der Ruf. Eine deutsche Nachkriegszeitschrift* (Deutscher Taschenbuch Verlag-Dokuments: Munich, 1962), p. 7. *Der Ruf* is hereafter cited as R. Schwab-Felisch (R 12) and H. Friedrich also report on the "suppression" itself (A 17). Letter of Curt Vinz to the author, dated May 1, 1969.

[4]Among the later political activities under the auspices of Group 47, mention should be made of the Grünwalder Kreis [Grünwald Circle]. Waldemar von Knöringen, State Chairman of the SPD in Bavaria, had invited interested persons to meet in the School for Athletics in Grünwald near Munich. The Circle was led by Dr. Vogel, G. Scszesny, and Hans Werner Richter. It held meetings in Munich, Cologne, Hamburg, and Berlin. "Richter let it die out when it became apparent that, to continue it, an organization was necessary for which the funds were lacking. The attempt, methods, and rules whereby Group 47 had hoped to exercise political influence had proved unsuccessful" (H 446). In April, 1958, the *Komitee gegen Atomrüstung* [Committee against Atomic Armament] was founded in Munich. Most of the participants, among them H. W. Richter and G. Scszesny, were from Group 47, but Gertrud von Le Fort and Erich Kästner were also present. During the federal elections in 1965, a dozen or so young authors, under the guidance of Grass and Richter, offered their services in setting up the election office of the SPD. The directors of the election office were K. Wagenbach and K. Roehler. On the subject of the direct engagement of writers in behalf of the existing parties, see Carl Amery, "Nach der Bundestagswahl," in *Fragen an Welt und Kirche* (Hamburg, 1967).

[5]The fall meeting of the Group in 1968 was supposed to take place in Czechoslovakia, but the political changes in Prague made it impossible to meet there. For the first time in its history, the Group held no meeting.

[6]After his attack on Herburger's and Höllerer's prose, Handke was not invited to the next meeting—a clear evidence of the degree of freedom and tolerance to be found in the Group. The invitation from Hans Werner Richter is, as everyone knows, a problematical affair. In the opinion of Heinrich Böll, sympathies, antipathies, whim, chance, even arbitrariness were not excluded as motives. "Withdrawal of the invitation did not depend on literary quality alone. . . . Some authors without a trace of genuine literary talent are invited again and again and come again and again. Others, as was their privilege, took the criticism personally and remained away; the after-effects of such injured feelings can be seen even today in the writings of some journalists and publicists" (Böll, H 392).

## Chapter 5

*Chapter 5*

[1]Heinrich Böll, *Aufsätze, Reden, Kritiken* (Cologne and Berlin, 1967), p. 234.

[2]James Baldwin, *Hundert Jahre Freiheit ohne Gleichberechtigung* (Hamburg, 1964), p. 51 f. James Joyce, *Stephen Daedalus* [Eng. title: *Stephen Hero*] (Fischer-Taschenbuch: Frankfurt, 1966), p. 52.

[3]In the German text, Leslie, Colum, Larbaud, and Buchholz are quoted from "Literatur vor Gericht," in *Akzente* (1965), pp. 210–251; quotations are from pp. 232 ff., 244. For an account of the proceedings against Sternheim's *Ulrike*, see Carl Sternheim, *Werke*, ed. Wilhelm Emrich, Vol. VI (Neuwied, 1966), p. 87 f. and 520 f.

Sixty years ago, when Catholicism was predominantly apologetic, a theologian whose horizon was delimited by an attitude learned from late Scholasticism and apologetics could write against a man like Carl Muth and his publications: "In a time when millions have turned aside from the light of the holy Catholic faith, when learned Sophists play with the name of the Savior of the world as though He had been an empty failure, when rationalism and pantheism are driving Christianity completely out of science and life, when literature ridicules all discipline and morality, when the triumph of nakedness in art and life is proclaiming the deepest moral degradation, then it is certainly opportune to remind one's fellowmen by clear and firm programs of the lofty goals of life and literature, to gather them together for practical activity, and, above all, to remind the degraded revolutionary spirit of the age of the eternal limits set upon intellectual as well as moral and aesthetic life." (A. Baumgartner, S. J., "Die katholische Belletristrik und die Moderne," in *Stimmen aus Maria Laach*, Vol. 77 [1909], p. 131.)

It is not our task and scarcely our right to sit in judgment on such sentences. What we are attempting is merely to point out a change in attitude.

[4]See Sartre, *Ist der Existentialismus Humanismus?*, Ullstein Book, no. 304 (Frankfurt and Berlin, 1966), p. 18. Bertolt Brecht, *Gesammelte Werke* (Suhrkamp: Frankfurt, 1967), Vol. 8, p. 54 ("Hymne an Gott"); pp. 187 ff. ("Bericht vom Zeck" [Zeck = Zecke (Eng. "tick") = the God of Christianity]). See also the scene "Gefängniszelle" [Prison Cell] in the first two versions of *Baal* (1918 and 1919), where Baal speaks with the clergyman (Suhrkamp, vol. no. 170).

[5]Baldwin, p. 83; Böll, p. 237.

[6]Baldwin, pp. 21, 56.

[7]See Oswald Loretz, *Galilei und der Irrtum der Inquisition* (Kevelaer, 1966), pp. 143 ff.: "The Silent Revision of the Church's Attitude toward Galileo in Vatican Council II." Brecht, *Gesammelte Werke*, Vol. 3, 1324.

[8]See Carl Amery [pseud. of Christian Mayer], *Die Provinz* (Deutscher Taschenbuch Verlag: Munich, 1964).———, *Die Kapitulation oder Deutscher Katholizismus heute* (Hamburg, 1963).———, *Fragen an Welt und Kirche* (Hamburg, 1967).

[9]Siegfried Lenz, *In Sachen Böll*, ed. Marcel Reich-Ranicki (Cologne, 1968), p. 41.

[10]*Hochland* 29/I (1931–1932), p. 183. But the same volume of the same journal also contains a defense of Brecht's *Hauspostille:* "However anti-Christian it may be, we cannot call a work Satanic when it brings us to such salutary self-examination" (Karl Thieme, p. 413).

Among writers in German, Hermann Broch was the first to take cognizance of the problem of knowledge in "closed" and "open" systems. See the essays "Zerfall der Werte" and "Das System als Welt-Bewältigung" in *Erkennen und Handeln*, Vol. 7 of the *Gesammelte Werke* (Zurich, 1955).

[11]Friedrich Dürrenmatt, *Theaterschriften und Reden* (Zurich, 1966), p. 123. Max Frisch, *Tagebuch* (Frankfurt, 1950), p. 195.

[12]Martin Walser, *Halbzeit* (Knaur-Taschenbuchausgabe: Munich, 1964), p. 247. Friedrich Dürrenmatt, *Komödien II* (Zurich, 1963), p. 311.

[13]Günter Eich in *Mein Gedicht ist mein Messer*, ed. Hans Bender (Munich, 1964), p. 23.

[14]Arno Schmidt in *Was halten Sie vom Christentum*, ed. K. Deschner (Munich, 1961), pp. 64 ff.

[15]The German text reads as follows:

*Gebet*
Grosser Gott auch von Biafra,
gütiger Gott aller Kinder,
von denen Du willst,
dass sie zu Dir kommen–
Schicke mehr Migs, dass sie es rascher können,
mehr Skodawaffen schicke, viel mehr,
auch Oerlikon, Vickers, Mauser, FN,
um ihren Weg zu Dir
zu verkürzen.

Schick einen Himmel voll,
aus Deinen Himmeln
einen voll Napalm,
dass alles schneller verbrennt,
die leichten Kokoshütten,
die Grassavanne,
die heimlichen Trampelpfade
von Milchpulvernachschub
für den unerbetenen Nachschub der Ibos.
Wir stiften Dir auch
vom reinen Öl aus Onitsha
für Dein Ewiges Licht.

[16]See G. Zwerenz in *Schwierigkeiten heute die Wahrheit zu schreiben*, ed. H. Friedrich (Munich, 1964), pp. 172 f.

[17]Goethe, *Werke* (Hamburg edition), Vol. 12, p. 392. Thomas Mann, *Betrachtungen eines Unpolitischen* (Stockholm edition: Frankfurt, 1956), p. 482.

[18]Quoted in H. Domin, *Wozu Lyrik heute* (Munich, 1968), p. 97.

[19]Gottfried Benn, *Gesammelte Werke* (Wiesbaden, 1958–1961), III, p. 320.

# *Index*